Sporting Questions Parrott Fashion

The Ultimate Trivial Challenge

John Parrott

Robson Books

First published in Great Britain in 2000
by Robson Books, 10 Blenheim Court, Brewery Road,
London N7 9NT

A member of the Chrysalis Group plc

British Library Cataloguing in Publicaiton Data
A catalogue record for this title is available from the
British Library

ISBN 1 86105 365 7

Printed in Great Britain by Bell & Bain Ltd., Glasgow

Contents

Foreword

Hello, and welcome to a sports quiz with a difference. You'll need a pen and paper for some questions, you can pit yourself against others in a snooker-style competition, and you'll keep sports enthusiasts busy with the multiple queries.

As a seven-year old my school report remarked, 'John would be far better served by reading a far better variety of books than the sports books he keeps his head buried in.' Fair comment but being a Merseysider my head has always been full of sporting trivia, as you've witnessed on *A Question of Sport*. I even get some right!

My main interests are football – and Everton in particular – snooker, horse racing and golf. My finest memories on the sporting field are undoubtedly of my snooker World championship win in 1991 when I bought a new cue just a month before the tournament started. I was invited to show the trophy off at Anfield, which I did, but if Everton had been at home then Goodison Park would have witnessed the only trophy won on Merseyside that year! Why do I support Everton? Well, my father took me there when the Blues defeated a Man Utd side containing the legendary George Best.

I tried all sports as a youngster but found snooker was the one in which I showed real aptitude at the age of thirteen. At sixteen I won BBC TV's Junior Pot Black in 1980 and I turned professional in 1984. Sport has helped me to see the world, meet *your* heroes and mine and to become a team captain on *the* quiz of them all – *A Question of Sport,* where I have shared many a laugh with 'supersub' Ally McCoist. Quizzes are a must on the snooker circuit as they help to liven up the quiet periods when we're not playing. John Higgins is one of many players who loves to pit his wits against others.

Q of S' Dave Ball, a member of the production team, has helped me in this collection of teasers. He was a former BBC Brain of Sport, is a Liverpool supporter and has worked on this show for over 15 years. Fellow

Evertonian Gavin Buckland is responsible for many of the snippets at the end of the book.

So, in the words of Magnus Magnusson, 'I've started so I'll finish' – now it's your turn.

Good luck and happy quizzing.

The Snooker Break

Here's your chance to play against yourself or against a friend. All you have to do is to 'pot' a red for a point then move on to the yellow (2 points), green (points), brown (4 points), blue (5 points), pink (6 points), and, if you are that good, the black gains you 7 points. That maximum will also give you a further 7 points, so there's 35 points on offer. If you fail on any ball then your opponents can start on the red, etc.

Naturally, the easier the question the fewer points you gain. So, off you go and happy 'potting'.

Red

1. Football
Which club was defeated in both FA Cup and
League Cup finals in 1997?

2. Snooker
In which city did John Higgins win his first world
title?

3. General
How many people are there in a volleyball team?

4. Football
Nicknamed 'Sparky', he became Wales' manager
in August 1999 – who is he?

5. General
How many people are there in an American
Football team?

6. Snooker
Which multi-world champion is nicknamed 'the
Nugget' and comes from Romford?

7. Football
Which player scored over 200 Premier League
goals for Rangers before joining Kilmarnock?

8. Cricket
Which country do England play in the Ashes series?

9. Horse Racing
On which racecourse is the Grand National run?

10. Athletics
In which event did Linford Christie win an Olympic Gold medal?

11. General
In which sport did Britain play USA for the Wightman Cup?

12. Football
Which First Division side lost in both FA Cup and Worthing Cup semi-finals in 1999-2000?

13. Cricket
Which country won the last World Cup Final?

14. Athletics
Which Briton has won two world 110 metres hurdles titles?

15. Football
Which 42-year-old goalkeeper played in the Premiership in 1999-2000 for Coventry City?

16. Motor Racing
Which circuit staged the 2000 British Grand Prix?

17. Rugby Union
Which country joined the Nations Tournament in 2000, the sixth side in the competition?

18. Rugby League
Who are the New Zealand brothers who play for Bradford Bulls?

19. Golf
Who was the Fijian who won the US Masters in 2000?

20. Football
Who in March 2000 became Liverpool's costliest player at 11 million?

21. Football
Who scored both Leicester's goals in the 2000 Worthington Cup Final?

22. Snooker
Which player was aiming for his eighth world title in 2000 but was knocked out in the first round?

23. Tennis
Which player won the most men's singles at Wimbledon in the 1990s?

24. Tennis
In which country was Greg Rusedski born?

25. Football
Who was voted both the European and World Player of the Year for 1999?

26. Horse Racing
Which racecourse stages the Derby in England?

27. Athletics
In which event did Jonathan Edwards set a world record?

28. Motor Racing
Which driver won the world title in both 1998 and 1999 in Formula 1?

29. Rugby Union
Which country defeated France to win the 1999

World Cup?

30. Rugby League
Which club sacked coach Ellery Hanley in 2000?

31. Golf
Who was the Briton who was a surprise winner of the Open in 1999 at Carnoustie?

32. Horse Racing
Which woman trainer had a second Grand National success in 1995 on 40-1 short Royal Athlete?

33. Motor Racing
Who in 1997 became the first Canadian Formula One world champion?

34. Football
Which Rangers legend was signed by Nottingham Forest in March 1999 on loan from San Jose Clash, and then joined Everton?

35. Rugby Union
Which country won the World Cup in June 1995 with a late drop goal from Joe Stransky?

36. Rugby League
Which club won the Challenge Cup for the eighth successive time in 1995?

37. Golf
Who in the 1990s won three US Amateur titles and then won a professional title in only his fifth event?

38. Football
Against which country did England lose for the first time under Kevin Keegan?

39. Tennis
What nationality is Bjorn Borg?

40. Athletics
Which hurdler became the first Briton to win a second world title in 1999?

41. Snooker
Which Welshman did Stephen Hendry defeat in the 1999 World Championship final at the Crucible?

42. Tennis
Who in 1987 was the last Australian to win the men's Wimbledon singles in the twentieth century?

43. Football
Who in 1998 became England's youngest international player in the twentieth century?

44. General
In which sport could you win a Lonsdale Belt?

45. Cricket
Test cricket is played at Trent Bridge – but which county plays there?

46. Darts
Which former world champion's nickname is the Crafty Cockney?

47. Football
Name either of the Frenchman who scored FA Cup Final goals in the 1990s?

48. Athletics
Which great American won the 1996 Olympic men's 200 and 400 metres?

49. Boxing
How many minutes are there from the first to last bell in 12-round title fights, including the time between rounds?

50. Snooker
Which player is known as the Whirlwind?

51. Football
Name either of the sides in the Football League in 1999-2000 which began with the letter D?

52. Rugby League
Who are the Bulls?

53. Athletics
In which event did Sally Gunnel win a world title?

54. Rugby Union
Which country's team are known as the All Blacks?

55. Golf
In which Major tournament does the winner get to wear a Green Jacket?

56. Athletics
At the beginning of 2000, which 'celebrity' still held the British men's 400 metres hurdles record?

57. Football
Which Premiership footballer scored Romania's winner against England in the 1998 World Cup?

58. Basketball
Who in 1996 signed for LA Lakers on a seven-year contract worth $120 million?

59. Tennis
Who in 1990s became the first Swiss woman to win the ladies' singles at Wimbledon?

60. Snooker
What nationality is Ronnie O'Sullivan?

61. Horse Racing
Who rode the odds-on favourite Reams of Verse when it won the Oaks at Epsom in 1997?

62. Football
What colour does Dennis Bergkamp's national team play in?

63. Cricket
Against which country did Dominic Cork take a hat-trick in 1995?

64. Cricket
Who captained England in 52 Tests from 1993-1998?

65. Basketball
For which side did Magic Johnson win five NBA titles?

66. Football
How often are the World Cup Finals held?

67. Athletics
How many events make up the women's heptathlon?

68. Golf
What is the minimum number of holes that a Major tournament must be played over?

69. Rugby Union
Which recent England skipper assumed the captaincy when aged only 22?

70. Rugby Union
How many points are awarded for a conversion?

71. Golf
Who in 1999 captained Europe's Ryder Cup side?

72. Athletics
Which British woman won an Olympic gold medal in 1992 with a time of 52.23 seconds?

73. Football
Who scored a hat-trick in just 4 minutes 33 seconds against Arsenal for Liverpool in 1994?

74. Rugby League
What position does Wendell Sailor usually play?

75. Basketball
Which team won six out of eight NBA titles between 1991 and 1998?

76. Tennis
Who in 1994 became the first Spanish woman to win the Wimbledon singles title?

77. Football
Which goalkeeper was Brazil's hero in their 1998 World Cup penalty shoot-out defeat of Holland?

78. Snooker
In what capacity were John Williams and Len Ganley known to fans of the sport?

79. Horse Racing
In which country are Classics held in Chantilly?

80. Rugby League
What is London's rugby league club called?

81. Football
Who was the first Scotsman to win 100 international caps?

82. Athletics
In which event did Ashia Hansen of Great Britain win a world indoor title?

83. Golf
Which famous golfer was known as the Golden Bear?

84. Rugby Union
How many points is a try worth?

85. General
With which sport do you associate Dennis Rodman?

86. Motor Racing
What nationality is Mika Hakkinen?

87. Rugby Union
Which country's national team are the Wallabies?

88. Golf
Which former American Ryder Cup golfer was known as the Walrus?

89. Athletics
Which event did Scotsman Allan Wells win at the 1980 Olympic Games?

90. Football
Which club did Ian Wright play for in an FA Cup Final prior to doing so for Arsenal?

91. Rugby League
He played for Wigan on the wing in 2000 and is known as Billy Whizz – who is he?

92. Basketball
Which side did Shaquille O'Neal and Kobe Bryant play for in February 2000?

93. Tennis
Which major championship is held at Roland Garros?

94. Football
Who was the first player to score 100 goals in the Premiership?

95. Snooker
Which Liverpudlian was the first European Open champion?

96. Horse Racing
Which famous English jockey won four of the five English classics in 1970?

97. Rugby
How many more players are there in a rugby union side compared with a rugby league side?

98. Football
Who was the South African who scored twice for Manchester United against Vasco da Gama in 2000?

99. Athletics
In which event did Carl Lewis win Olympic Gold medals on four successive occasions?

100. Golf
Which American won the 1994 US Amateur title and three years later won the US Masters?

101. Basketball
By what name is Earvin Johnson better known?

102. Motor Racing
On which circuit is Woodcote Corner?

103. Rugby Union
In which position did Jason Leonard win a record number of caps for England?

104. Golf
Which Scottish course is known as the Old Lady?

105. Athletics
What nationality is Frankie Fredericks?

106. Football
For which country did Cesar Sempaio score the opening goal of the 1998 World Cup against Scotland?

107. Rugby League
Which club in the Super League are known as the Blue Sox?

108. Tennis
Where in the USA has the US Open been played since 1978?

109. Snooker
Two Englishmen in the 1980s won the world title – Steve Davis and who else?

110. Horse Racing
Besides the Derby, which other Classic is run at Epsom?

111. Football
Which then Premiership player scored both goals in France's 2-0 victory over England in February 1999?

112. Athletics
Who was the Briton who won consecutive Olympic 1500 metres titles in 1980s?

113. Motor Racing
Which UK driver won 31 Grands Prix between 1980 and 1995?

114. Basketball
How many people make up a basketball team?

115. Rugby Union
What is the nickname of the South African team?

116. Football
In which country would you be playing top class football in the Bundesliga?

117. General
François Pienaar was a World Cup-winning captain in which sport?

118. Horse Riding
What nationality is Steve Cauthen?

119. Tennis
Who are the American sisters, one of whom won the US Open singles final in 1999, whilst the other became Wimbledon's singles champion in 2000?

120. Snooker
Who in 1990 became the youngest world champion?

121. Basketball
Which famous player's alternative career is as a wrestler where he uses the name 'Godzilla'?

122. Rugby Union
By what name is the British Isles team known when playing on an overseas tour?

123. Golf
What nationality is Greg Norman?

124. Athletics
Which athlete won Britain's only 1996 Olympic medal in women's competition?

125. Football
Which English club won their first European Cup in 1977?

126. Rugby League
What was Bradford's Bulls' name from 1907-08 to 1995-6?

127. Athletics
American Dan O'Brien broke which Briton's world decathlon record?

128. Golf
Who was the Spaniard who won his first US Masters title in 1994 and his second in 1999?

129. Rugby Union
What does the term 'no side' mean?

130. Rugby Union
Where do Scotland play their home games?

131. Athletics
Which pole vaulter between 1984 and 1998 set 17 outdoor world records?

132. Snooker
How many frames does the world champion have to win in the final in order to claim the title?

133. Rugby League
A Welshman was voted the 1998 Man of Steel and Player of the Year – who is he?

134. General
With which sport do you associate Joe Montana?

135. General
In which sport do teams compete for the Ryder Cup?

136. Tennis
Who was the last Briton to win a Wimbledon singles title?

137. Rowing
Who were the brothers who won medals for Britain in both the 1992 and 1996 Olympic Games?

138. Football
Who captained France to victory in the 1998 World Cup Final?

139. General
Paul Palmer won two medals at the 1998 World Championships in which sport?

140. Rugby League
Where in Scotland was the 2000 Challenge Cup Final held?

141. Ice Hockey
Who is the Canadian who is the record points scorer in National Hockey League history?

142. Athletics
Which American broke five world records and equalled a sixth within 45 minutes in 1935?

143. Rugby Union
Who captained England to successive Grand Slam titles in 1991 and 1992?

144. Snooker
Which former world champion is known as Dracula?

145. Tennis
Who in 1999 became only the fifth man to have won all four Grand Slam singles titles?

146. Football
Who was the first Chelsea player to be voted Footballer of the Year by the football writers?

147. Football
Which Premiership side had the famous Holte End, containing over 13000 seats?

148. Boxing
Which legendary fighter was the first to win the world heavyweight title three times?

149. Rugby Union
What is the surname of the England Test wingers Rory and Tony?

150. Rugby League
Which club plays its home games at the JJB stadium?

151. Football
Who played in a losing FA Cup final replay in 1990 and 1993 with different clubs?

152. Snooker
How many red balls are used in a frame of snooker?

153. Cricket
Who was the England coach who left his position after the 1999 World Cup?

154. Horse Racing
What Horses of what age are permitted to run in the English Classics?

155. General
How many penalty points will a rider pick up in show jumping if he or she knocks down a fence?

156. General
Which team won gold in the men's basketball event at the 1996 Atlanta Games?

157. General
In which city would Storm be playing their home games in ice hockey?

158. Football
Who is the only player to score in three different FA Cup Finals at Wembley, doing so from 1986 to 1992?

159. Cricket
Who in 1994 scored a Test record 375 against England?

160. Boxing
Which fighter was born in Hungary and later adopted both Britain and Australia as his homeland?

161. Athletics
What is the maximum number of competitors allowed in a sprint final?

162. Snooker
What colour ball has a value of seven points when potted?

163. Horse Racing
On which course is the Prix de l'Arc de Triomphe run annually?

164. Motor Racing
Which country's Grand Prix circuit is named after Gilles Villeneuve?

165. Boxing
About which boxer did Mills Lane remark, 'One bite is bad enough, two is dessert'?

166. Cricket
Which country won the World Cup for the first time in 1992?

167. Golf
Costantino Rocca was the first player from which country to play Ryder Cup golf?

168. Tennis
Lleyton Hewitt is a new teenage sensation, but which country is he from?

169. Rugby Union
In which year was the Rugby World Cup first played?

170. Football
Who managed Sheffield Wednesday when they were defeated in two domestic Wembley Cup finals in 1993?

171. General
How high is the net in squash?

172. General
Which race starts and ends at Putney and Mortlake?

173. American Football
By what name was William Perry known?

174. Football
At which Premiership club would you find a manager, his assistant and a young midfielder all from the same family?

175. Cricket
Which legendary figure held the record number of Test appearances as an umpire on 1 January 2000?

176. Motor Racing
For which constructor did Michael Schumacher win his world title in 1995?

177. Horse Racing
Which National Hunt jockey retired in 1999 with a record 1,699 wins in Britain?

178. Football
Which was the last country to play in the final of three successive World Cups?

179. Cricket
What is Birmingham's Test match ground called?

180. Football
Which footballer was voted BBC Sports Personality of the Year in 1998?

181. Boxing
From which man did Evander Holyfield take the world heavyweight title for the first time in 1990?

182. Rowing
Who partnered Steve Redgrave in the Olympic coxless pairs in 1992 and 1996?

183. General
In which sport might you be penalised for 'travelling'?

184. General
How many people are there in a netball team?

185. Golf
Which Spaniard won his third British Open in 1988 at Lytham?

186. Football
Which Premiership manager in 1999-2000 had captained England 65 times?

187. Boxing
How many minutes' duration is a round in professional boxing?

188. Football
Which West Ham player was capped at the age of 19 years in the 1990s?

189. Boxing
Who in 1998 became the first British woman to contest a professional bout in this country?

190. Tennis
What is the surname of the brothers Luke and Murphy, famous for their doubles play?

191. Cricket
Who took over the Australian captaincy from his brother Ian?

192. Athletics
Which athlete won the 1988 Olympic 100 metres only to be disqualified for a drug offence?

193. Football
Besides Juventus, which other club has Didier Deschamps played for in a European Cup Final?

194. Cricket
Which New Zealander was knighted by the Queen before retiring from Test cricket?

195. Motor Racing
Eddie Irvine won the opening Grand Prix of 1999 – which Grand Prix was this?

196. Golf
What does a golfer shout to another to warn of any danger of being hit?

197. Horse Racing
Where are the 1,000 Guineas and 2,000 Guineas run annually?

198. Boxing
In the Olympic Games, which is the heaviest weight category?

199. Cricket
Who was the first spinner to take 300 Test wickets for Australia?

200. General
In which sport in Britain's James Cracknell a world champion?

201. General
Joanne Conway was six times British champion in which sport?

202. Football
Who was the first manager from outside the British Isles to win the English Championship?

203. Boxing
At which weight did Herbie Hide once hold a world title?

204. Cricket
At which ground were the first three World Cup Finals Held?

205. Athletics
How many hurdles are there in the 400 metres hurdles?

206. Horse Racing
Kieren Fallon won three English Classics in 1999, but who trained all three winners?

207. Motor Racing
Which driver won the opening three Grands Prix in 2000?

208. Boxing
Which former British heavyweight champion of the 1970s won a world title in Brisbane in 1998?

209. Tennis
Which Czech player played in eight successive US Open men's singles finals in the 1980s?

210. Motor Racing
How many points does the winner of a Grand Prix score?

211. Cricket
Which Englishman famously swore at umpire Shakoor Rana during a Test match?

212. General
In which sport did Phil Taylor win his seventh world title in 1999?

213. General
With which sport do you associate Gigi Fernandez?

214. Football
Which goalkeeper returned to the Premiership in 1999-2000 for Bradford City, aged over 40?

215. General
In which Texan city is the Astrodome where many major sporting events are promoted?

216. Motor Racing
Which legendary Scottish driver won the World Championship in 1969, 1971 and 1973?

217. Rugby Union
Who was the Bath player appointed Will Carling's successor as England captain in 1996?

218. Football
Who took over from Bobby Robson as manager of England in 1990?

219. General
With which sport do you associate the charismatic Don King?

220. Tennis
Which country provided both of the men's singles finalists at Wimbledon in 1991?

221. Boxing
Nicknamed Big Daddy, this American held the IBF, WBA and WBC world heavyweight titles in 1992 – who is he?

222. Football
Which London Premiership club has had only eight managers since 1900?

223. General
With which sport do you associate the Cresta Run?

224. Motor racing
Who is the 19-year old Briton who made his Formula One debut in 2000?

225. Cricket
Which country did South African Allan Donald play for in 2000?

226. Football
Which footballer had a hit with 'Head Over Heels' in 1979 and in 2000 was a well-known manager?

227. General
In which sport is Peter Nicol a world champion?

228. Horse Racing
Which horse won the Champion Hurdle for the third time in 2000?

229. Football
Which current Premiership manager was once in charge of Japanese club Nagoya Grampus Eight?

230. Football
Which club in 1992 became the first to reach a second post-war FA Cup Final while playing in the Second Division?

231. General
In which sport was Geoff Capes a British No.1 from 1970 to 1980 and World No.1 in 1975?

232. Football
Man United completed the Double in 1994 – but which side prevented their Treble by beating them in the League Cup Final?

233. General
Which country staged the 1996 Olympic Games?

234. Horse Racing
Who at the age of 56 rode his 30th British Classic winner in 1992 on Rodrigo de Triano?

235. Athletics
Who in 1992 took just 9.96 seconds to win Olympic gold in Barcelona?

236. Motor Racing
Who in 1992 achieved pole position a record fourteen times and won nine of the races to win his only World Championship?

237. Football
For which club was Karl-Heinz Riedle playing when he scored twice in the 1997 European Cup Final?

238. American Football
Name the 300-1 winners of the 2000 Super Bowl, who beat Tennessee Titans?

239. Rugby Union
Who was the last Englishman to captain the British Lions?

240. Tennis
Who was the world No 1 woman player who was stabbed by a spectator in Hamburg in May 1993?

241. Boxing
Who in 1994 won the world heavyweight title at the age of 46?

242. Football
Which country came in as a late replacement and won the 1992 European Championship?

243. General
In which sport do players play with a shuttlecock?

244. Football
Who in 1999-2000 broke Paul McGrath's record as the Republic of Ireland's most capped player?

245. Snooker
Who won his first world snooker title in 2000?

246. Horse Racing
Which exuberant jockey rode seven winners in a day at Ascot in 1996?

247. Football
Who in 1997 scored Italy's winner against England and inflicted upon England their first World Cup defeat at Wembley?

248. General
Which is the most prestigious cycle race in Europe?

249. General
In 1981 Neil Adams became the first British male to win a world title in which sport?

250. Football
Who scored the winning goal in the last minute of the 1993 FA Cup Final replay?

251. Motor Racing
For the first time in twelve years a driver died at a Grand Prix in 1994. Which three times world champion died in the San Marino GP?

252. Rugby Union
In 1998 which player played for England at full back, fly half, and on the wing?

253. Rugby League
Which winger moved from Widnes to Wigan for a world record £440,000 in 1992?

254. Football
Besides Liverpool, which other club did Kevin Keegan play for in a European Cup Final?

255. General
Which major race passed over British soil for only the second time in its 91-year history in 1994?

256. Tennis
Who was the only German to win the men's singles title at Wimbledon in the 1990s?

257. Boxing
At which weight did Lloyd Honeyghan score a surprise win over the world champion Don Curry in 1986?

258. Football
Name either of the English-born managers who won the FA Cup in the 1990s?

259. General
With which sport do you associate the Jules Rimet Trophy?

260. Horse Racing
Which mother and son won the 1991 Cheltenham Gold Cup as trainer and jockey?

261. Motor Racing
In the 1950s, which British driver was runner-up in the World Championship for four consecutive years?

262. Rugby Union
Who is the only British player to score over 800 points in internationals?

263. Tennis
Pat Rafter beat which Briton to win the US Open singles in 1997?

264. Boxing
Who in 1993 was given the WBC heavyweight title

after Riddick Bowe relinquished it and threw the
championship belt in a rubbish bin?

265. Cricket
Which county did Shane Warne play for in 2000?

266. Football
Which 2000 Premiership manager captained the
1992 League Championship winners?

267. General
What famous race did Bernard Hinault win for the
fifth and final time in 1985?

268. General
In 1984 which pair achieved the highest scores in
Olympic ice skating history?

269. Horse Racing
Which jockey rode Shergar, Shahrastani and
Lammtarra to Derby success?

270. Tennis
Which Czech won eight Grand Slam singles titles in
the Eighties and Nineties, but never won
Wimbledon?

271. Football
For which club did Ian Rush score his League Cup
record-equalling 49th goal in 1997?

272. Snooker
Prior to Mark Williams in 1999, who was the last
Welshman to reach a World Championship final?

273. General
With which sport do you associate Dennis
Priestley?

274. Horse Racing
In which annual race do horses face the Chair and Bechers Brook?

275. Football
Which club did Liverpool defeat to win their only FA Cup in the 1970s?

276. Athletics
Mike Powell broke Bob Beamon's world record in 1991, which had stood for 23 years – but which event was this?

277. Motor Racing
Which circuit is known as the Brickyard?

278. Rugby Union
England appeared in their first World Cup Final in 1991 – which country defeated them?

279. Rugby League
Which of the Paul brothers scored three tries in the 1996 Challenge Cup Final yet still finished on the losing side?

280. General
Which American football team play at Mile High Stadium?

281. General
What equestrian event is held annually at the All-England Jumping Centre at Hickstead in Sussex?

282. Football
Match of the Day commentator Garth Crooks played for which club in an FA Cup Final in 1981?

283. General
Which sport normally starts between one and five and finishes between seven and eight?

284. General
In which sport do teams play with a puck?

285. Football
Who played for three Italian clubs in the 1990s and won FA Cup and Premiership winners' medals in 1998?

286. Motor Racing
Which country staged the opening round of the 2000 World Championship?

287. General
In which city are the Seahawks American football team based?

288. Football
Who played for Liverpool in 1999-2000 and in 1994 became the third youngest World Cup player in the final stages?

289. Motor Racing
Who were the first father and son to win the world drivers' title (they were British)?

290. Football
Who scored Scotland's only goal in Euro 1996?

291. Horse Racing
On which course would you have to negotiate Tattenham Corner?

292. Rugby Union
Who captained England in their 1991 World Cup Final defeat?

293. Tennis
Who in 1992 became the USA's first Wimbledon men's singles champion since John McEnroe in 1984?

294. Boxing
Who in 1994 was the Norwich-based heavyweight who won the WBO title by defeating Michael Bentt in England?

295. Football
Who was the last man to manage different sides to the League title?

296. General
From which show did Torvill and Dean take their popular routine featuring a circus theme?

297. Motor Racing
Who in 1993 became the first man ever to follow a Formula One title with an IndyCar Championship in successive years?

298. Cricket
Which county captained by Matthew Maynard surprisingly won the County Championship in 1997?

299. Darts
Which Englishman won the world title in 1979 and 1987?

300. Football
Which Italian club did Paul Gascoigne play for?

Yellow

1. Football
Who was the only Dutchman to score in an FA Cup Final in the 1990s?

2. Athletics
Which event did Briton Tessa Sanderson win in the 1984 Olympic Games?

3. Olympics
In which Asian city were the 1988 Summer Games held?

4. Football
Who in the 1990s became the first manager to win the FA Cup four times with the same club?

5. General
In which sport do England play Scotland for the Calcutta Cup?

6. Cricket
Which West Indian bowler broke the world record for the most Test dismissals in 2000?

7. Football
Name the two Channel Islanders who've played for England (they're still in the Premiership).

8. Boxing
Which Briton in 2000 held the WBO world featherweight title?

9. Horse Racing
Where is the Champion Hurdle run?

10. Football
Who was the first Englishman to be sent off in an international at Wembley?

11. Snooker
Who was the Hong Kong player knocked out in round one of the World Championships in 2000?

12. Horse Riding
Who in February 2000 became the first trainer to saddle 3,000 winners in National Hunt history?

13. Football
Roy Keane has played in five FA Cup Finals – but which club was he with on the first occasion?

14. Motor Racing
Which British driver won the British Grand Prix in both 1999 and 2000?

15. Rugby Union
Which Briton was the individual leading scorer in the Six Nations tournament in 2000?

16. Rugby League
Which club has won the Challenge Cup on the most occasions?

17. Football
Which then Everton player scored against England at Wembley in 1999-2000?

18. Cricket
Who on 24 June 1999 became the England Test captain?

19. Boxing
Which former world champion defeated British heavyweight champion Julius Francis in January 2000 in Manchester?

20. Football
Which club was defeated on two occasions in the FA Cup in 1999-2000?

21. Football
Which country did Germany defeat to win their third European Championship in 1996?

22. Golf
Which Briton topped the European Order of Merit for most of the 1990s?

23. Boxing
Which legend rose to prominence when winning the Olympic light-heavyweight title in 1960?

24. General
In which sport did Tommi Makinen win a hat-trick of world titles?

25. Football
Who scored both of Germany's goals in the 1996 European Championship final, including the Golden Goal decider?

26. Tennis
Who was the last Briton to reach a grand slam singles final prior to 2000?

27. Snooker
Which legendary Irishman was known as the

Hurricane?

28. Motor Racing
Which Briton won his only world title in a McLaren in 1976?

29. Athletics
Who in the 1990s became the first British woman to win World and Olympic titles?

30. Football
Who were the cousins in England's 1998 World Cup squad?

31. Rugby Union
Which winger has scored the most tries for Wales?

32. Football
Which player started the 1999-2000 season by scoring last-minute own goals.

33. Cricket
Against which nation do England play for the Wisden Trophy?

34. Boxing
Which Briton in 1995 finally won the WBC heavyweight title against Oliver McCall?

35. Horse Racing
Which is the only horse to win the Aintree Grand National on three occasions?

36. Athletics
In which event did Javier Sotomayor break world records?

37. Football
Who was the Italian who missed the final penalty which gave Brazil the World Cup in 1994?

38. Golf
Who is the only man with a hyphen in his surname to win the Open?

39. Motor Racing
Which make of car did Nigel Mansell, Alain Prost and Damon Hill all drive to win the world title in the 1990s?

40. Football
Which legendary player captained West Germany to victory in the 1990 World Cup and played throughout the 1990s?

41. Athletics
By what nickname was Florence Griffith Joyner better known?

42. Tennis
Who won the Wimbledon men's singles every year from 1976 to 1980?

43. Football
Who was the last man to score twice in a World Cup final?

44. Motor Racing
Alain Prost was the first driver from which country to win the world title?

45. Boxing
Who was the Welshman who won the world featherweight crown in the 1990s?

46. Snooker
How many points are usually needed to constitute a maximum break?

47. Cricket
On which Test ground do Surrey play their home

matches?

48. Football
Who was the last person in the twentieth century to manage two different FA Cup final losing sides, doing so in 1988 and 1998?

49. Horse Racing
Which legendary jockey won nine Epsom Derbys, his first in 1954?

50. Rugby Union
In 1998 which fly half made his England debut at the age of 18?

51. Golf
Which golfer is known as the Wild Thing?

52. Football
Name the two England managers who have also managed Barcelona.

53. American Football
Which side won their first ever Super Bowl in 1998?

54. Swimming
David Wilkie and Duncan Goodhew both won Olympic titles at which stroke?

55. Golf
Who in 1996 became the first British sportswoman to earn over £1 million in a year?

56. Football
Who scored the only hat-trick in the 1998 World Cup finals?

57. Rugby League
Name either of the sides which contested the Challenge Cup Final in 2000.

58. Cricket
Who by January 2000 had played in most Tests for Australia and captained them on the most occasions?

59. Rugby Union
In which position did Jeremy Guscott and Will Carling play for England?

60. Athletics
In which event did British-born Fiona May win a world title for Italy in 1995?

61. Tennis
Which Australian retained his men's US Open singles title in 1998?

62. Football
Who played for Ipswich in the 1981 UEFA Cup final and Ajax in the 1988 Cup-Winners' Cup final?

63. General
What do the initials IOC stand for?

64. General
These brothers play for England at football and their sister represents England at netball – name the family.

65. Basketball
For which side did Magic Johnson win five NBA titles?

66. Football
Who in 1988 aged only 17 became the youngest player to hit a top flight hat-trick in the League?

67. Rugby Union
Which country did South Africa defeat to win the 1995 World Cup Final?

68. Horse Riding
Which horse came second in both the 1997 and 1998 Grand National?

69. Snooker
Which Englishman won the World Championship on six occasions and in January 2000 was ranked world No. 15?

70. Motor Racing
Who was the Formula One world champion in both 1994 and 1995?

1. Rugby Union
Who captained the victorious British Lions in South Africa in 1997?

2. Football
Which club was defeated in both the FA Cup and League Cup Finals in 1993?

3. Snooker
Jimmy White lost in six World Championship Finals, but who defeated him in his first final in 1984?

4. Horse Racing
Which horse won the Grand National the last time it was run on a Monday?

5. Darts
Name the Limestone Cowboy who won the world title for the only time in 1988?

6. Football
Which then Premiership goalkeeper scored in a European game against Rotor Volgograd in the 1990s?

7. Cricket
Who was the last Englishman to score a Test

triple century?

8. Athletics
Prior to Linford Christie, who was the last Briton to win the Olympic 100 metres?

9. Rugby League
Which player is nicknamed Chariots?

10. Football
Which was the last African nation to be defeated in the 1998 World Cup?

11. Rugby Union
Whose drop goal sealed the British Lions' series win in the second Test against South Africa in 1977?

12. Ice Skating
Name either of the Britons who've won post-war Olympic gold medals in the men's events?

13. Football
Known as the Indomitable Lions, they qualified for the 1982, 1990, 1994 and 1998 World Cup Finals – name them.

14. Boxing
Who was the Irishman who ended Chris Eubank's 43-fight unbeaten record to become WBO super-middleweight world champion?

15. Motor Racing
Which Briton won four Grands Prix and finished as World Championship runner-up in 1999?

16. Golf
Who in 1999 became the youngest ever Ryder Cup player?

17. Football
Who in 1990 scored a penalty to win the World Cup for Germany?

18. Football
Which club won successive European Cups in 1989 and 1990?

19. Cricket
Which Australian in 1999 became the first to score a century against all eight Test playing countries?

20. Horse Racing
Which Liverpudlian 'funny man' owned the 1994 Grand National winner Miinnehoma?

21. Motor Cycling
Who was the last Briton to win the world 500cc title?

22. Golf
Who was the first Briton to win the British Open in the 1990s?

23. Football
Who was the last Englishman to manage a League Championship winning side prior to 2000?

24. Horse Racing
Which horse did Willie Carson ride to victory in the 1989 Derby and 2,000 Guineas?

25. Darts
What is the lowest score you can not make with a single dart?

26. Rugby League
Which club's nickname is the Wolves?

27. Football
Between 1845 and 2000, only one club won three successive League titles – who are they?

28. General
Which British city hosted the 1970 and 1986 Commonwealth Games?

29. General
In which sport have Britons Michael Lee and Gary Havelock been world champions?

30. Athletics
Which British male high jumper won European silver and Commonwealth gold in 1998?

31. Cricket
Who by 1 January 2000 was England's highest run scorer in Test matches?

32. Rugby Union
Who in 1999 scored a try for Scotland within nine seconds of the start against Wales?

33. Football
Which 1996 World Cup winner managed Newcastle, Middlesbrough and Sheffield Wednesday?

34. Horse Racing
On which racecourse are the Irish Classics run?

35. Rugby League
John Kear coached which club to their first Challenge Cup Final victory in 1998?

36. Golf
Which South African twice won the US Open in the 1990s?

37. General
In which sport would play on a diamond?

38. Football
Who in 1988 became the first goalkeeper to captain the FA Cup winning team?

39. Boxing
Who was the first man to defeat Lennox Lewis in a professional contest?

40. Tennis
Which woman won the Wimbledon singles seven times between 1988 and 1996?

41. Olympics
In which sport did Britain gain their only gold medal in the Atlanta Games?

42. Rugby Union
In which other sport did Nigel Walker of Wales compete at international level?

43. Football
Whose last game for England was in the 1992 European Championship finals against Sweden, finishing with 48 goals in his career?

44. Football
Who managed Manchester United prior to Alex Ferguson?

45. General
Who in 1988 partnered Briton Andrew Holmes to Olympic gold?

46. Athletics
Which British woman won the World Championship 10,000 metres in 1991?

47. Boxing
Which Briton lost in world title fights to Tyson, Lewis and Witherspoon?

48. Rugby
In 1995 which legendary Welshman returned to rugby union with Cardiff after spells with Widnes and Warrington in rugby league?

49. Football
Which former Tottenham player scored the goal which defeated Arsenal in the 1995 Cup-Winners' Cup Final?

50. Golf
On which golf course did Europe defeat the Americans in the 1997 Ryder Cup?

51. General
In which sport did Michael Doohan win his third successive world title in 1996?

52. Olympics
In which American city were the Olympic Games held in 1984?

53. Horse Racing
Which famous jockey has ridden the most English Classic winners?

54. Football
Which player has scored the most goals for England?

55. Football
Against which country did Gary Lineker score two goals from the penalty spot in the 1990 World Cup?

56. Rugby Union
Who scored two tries on his England debut in 2000 and is the nephew of an England footballer?

57. Snooker
Who in February 2000 missed the black and so failed to achieve a maximum in the B&H Masters?

58. Golf
Which American won his fifth British Open in 1983?

59. Olympics
Which country staged the 1998 Winter Games?

60. General
In which sport do you compete in slalom, tricks and jumps?

61. Motor Sport
Who was Britain's first world rally champion?

62. Golf
Which American won the US Open in 1988 and 1989?

63. Horse Racing
Which horse won the Triple Crown in 1970?

64. Basketball
What do the letters MVP stand for?

65. Athletics
Which British woman won a World Championship medal in the 1500 metres and 800 metres in 1995?

66. Cricket
Who was the non-striker whose run-out blunder against Australia cost South Africa a place in the

1999 World Cup Final?

67. Football
Which club were originally banned from the 1995 FA Cup, but were reinstated and reached the semi-finals?

68. Cricket
Can you name the Scotsman who captained England in Tests in the 1970s?

69. Motor Racing
Which British world champion won a then record 27 Grands Prix between 1965 and 1973?

70. Boxing
Under what name did Muhammad Ali win an Olympic gold medal?

1. Football
Who in 1993 became the first USA international to make an FA Cup Final appearance?

2. Snooker
Which player did John Parrott defeat to win his world title in 1991?

3. Cycling
Who was the Spaniard who won the Tour de France five times in succession in the 1990s?

4. Football
Name the Argentinian who scored the most goals in the 1978 World Cup finals?

5. Cricket
Who was the Lancashire player who captained West Indies to their 1975 World Cup win?

6. Horse Racing
Which jockey rode Party Politics and Earth Summit to Grand National victories?

7. Athletics
Which Briton won the Olympic 1500 metres in 1980 and 1984?

8. Football
Which player in the 1980s won a League Championship medal with both Everton and Arsenal?

9. Boxing
Who won a world title for the first time in November 1986 defeating Trevor Berbick?

10. Cricket
Who played in 131 Tests for India and took a then world record 434 wickets?

11. Tennis
Who was the only unseeded winner of the Wimbledon's men's singles in the 1990s?

12. Football
Which is the only country the Republic of Ireland have defeated in the World Cup finals, in open play?

13. Snooker
Who was the first player to win the world amateur and professional titles?

14. Football
Which is the only country to have played in all the final stages of all 16 World Cups?

15. General
With which sport do you associate the America's Cup?

16. Boxing
At which weight did Joe Calzaghe and Richie Woodhall both win world titles in 1997 and 1998 respectively?

17. Horse Racing
Who in 1983 became the first woman trainer of a Grand National winner?

18. Football
Who scored Scotland's opening goal in the World Cup in France?

19. Cricket
Who was the last bowler to take a hat-trick in an Ashes Test in the 1990s?

20. Athletics
Which British athlete's world record was broken in 1997 by Wilson Kipketer?

21. Football
Who is the only player to score two FA Cup Final penalties in the same game?

22. Football
Who captained Brazil to successive World Cup Finals in 1994 and 1998?

23. Athletics
Which famous athlete won his fourth successive individual Olympic title in a field event in 1996?

24. Cricket
Which New Zealander did the double in England in 1984 – 100 wickets and 1,000 runs?

25. General
What is historically 26 miles 385 yards in length?

26. Horse Racing
Which jockey rode three consecutive Arc de Triomphe winners in the 1990s.

27. Snooker
Who won the 1985 world title yet lost in round one in 1986 to Mike Hallet?

28. Football
Who scored England's first goal in the 1998 World Cup?

29. Athletics
Which British athlete won the 400 metres in the World Cup, European Championship and Commonwealth Games in 1998?

30. Golf
Who finished fourth equal in the Open at Birkdale in 1998 yet took home nothing of the £55,000 he could have won?

31. Tennis
After the tears of 1993, which veteran won the women's singles at Wimbledon for the first time in 1998?

32. Football
Which manager won the Scottish League title in 1998 and then quit?

33. Football
Which club in 1997-98 had three players sent off in a Premiership game against Liverpool?

34. Golf
Which course in Sutton Coldfield staged the Ryder Cup in 1985, 1989 and 1993?

35. Horse Racing
Which jockey rode Slip Anchor and Reference Point to Epsom Derby successes?

36. Baseball
How many people are there in a baseball team?

37. Football
Which Frenchman scored nine goals in the 1984 European championship finals and led his country to victory?

38. Tennis
Which British girl partnered Jeremy Bates to victory in the Wimbledon mixed doubles?

39. General
Welshman Leighton Rees was the first winner of which sport's world title in 1978?

40. Boxing
Who made 19 successful defences of the world heavyweight title between Muhammad Ali's final reign and Mike Tyson's accession?

41. Cricket
Who held 1473 catches behind the wicket for Derbyshire and England between 1960 and 1988?

42. Gymnastics
Who was the Russian who won gold medals in the women's beam and floor exercises at the 1972 Olympics?

43. Horse Racing
Who rode Red Rum to two of his Grand National victories?

44. Football
Which Liverpool player in 1999 won his record 22nd England under-21 cap, to go with his first full cap?

45. General
In which sport would you use a foil or an épée?

46. Boxing
Who in 1998 became the first fighter in four years to take Naseem Hamed the distance?

47. Athletics
Which Northern Ireland athlete won an Olympic gold medal in 1972 at Munich?

48. Golf
Who was the Briton whose only Championship success came in 1985?

49. General
With which sport would you associate the yellow jersey and the polka dot jersey?

50. Football
Who was the only Arsenal player in the 1990s to be named as the Footballer of the Year by the football writers?

51. Cricket
Which English bowler in 1997-8 took eight wickets in an innings against the West Indies for the second time in his career?

52. General
In which sport was Holland's Ray Barneveld his country's first world champion?

53. Tennis
Which player won her seventh Wimbledon title after beating Spanish player Arantxa Sanchez-Vicario in 1996?

54. Football
Which country did England defeat in the quarter-finals of Euro 96 on penalties?

55. Cricket
Who was the last batsman to complete a century of centuries, many of them with Worcestershire?

56. Football
Which German appeared in his fifth World Cup finals in 1998?

57. Golf
Which legendary post-war golfer has won the most Major tournaments?

58. Boxing
On which football ground did Barry McGuigan defeat Eusebio Pedroza in 1985 to win a world title?

59. Basketball
Which famous player is known as the Worm?

60. Golf
Which tournament was contested at Valderrama in 1997?

1. Football
Who was the Italian who won the Golden Boot in the 1990 World Cup finals?

2. Athletics
Who was the Italian who pipped Allan Wells to win the Olympic 200 metres in 1980?

3. Cricket
Which Australian in 1972 took 16 wickets for 137 in the Lord's test?

4. Football
From which club did Liverpool sign future England captains Kevin Keegan and Ray Clemence?

5. Tennis
Who partnered John McEnroe to four of his five Wimbledon men's doubles titles?

6. Boxing
Who was the Liverpool fighter who lost a world light-heavyweight title fight to Mate Parlov in the 1970s?

7. Football
Which player was sent off in the FA Cup semi-final at Wembley in 1993?

8. Horse Racing
Who rode the 1991 Gold Cup winner and just 23 days later was runner-up in the Grand National on the same horse?

9. Golf
Who was the only Briton to win the Open in the 1990s at Carnoustie?

10. Football
Prior to David Beckham, who was the last England player sent off in the World Cup finals?

11. Football
Which country made their World Cup debut in Italia 90 and beat Scotland in their first match?

12. Horse Racing
Who rode Aldaniti to victory in the 1981 Grand National?

13. Athletics
Which Briton defended his Olympic title in 1984, emulating compatriot Sebastian Coe?

14. Football
Name either of the two English clubs that won the UEFA Cup in the 1980s?

15. Motor Racing
Which man has won a record 51 Grands Prix, doing so from 1980 to 1993?

16. Rugby Union
In 1995 Rob Andrew became which club's first development director?

17. Rugby League
Name the scrum half who won nine Challenge Cup winners' medals?

18. Cricket
Which Australian hit a post-war record of 839 runs in the 1989 Ashes series?

19. Football
Who did Liverpool defeat to become the first side to win the European Cup on penalties?

20. General
With which sport do you associate the Stanley Cup?

21. Football
Who were the brothers who played for Holland in their 1988 European Championship win?

22. Rugby League
From which club did Leeds sign Welsh star Iestyn Harris?

23. Boxing
Who was the British light-heavyweight who won a world title for the third time in 1990?

24. General
In which sport would you expect to see competitors performing a Salchow?

25. Tennis
Who did the Romanian Bjorn Borg defeat to win his first Wimbledon singles title?

26. Football
Who managed Scotland during the 1978 World Cup finals?

27. Snooker
Silvino Francisco won the 1985 British Open, but what is his nationality?

28. General
In which sport did Graham Obree win a World Championship over 4,000 metres?

29. Bowls
Which Briton won the world outdoor bowls titles in 1992 and 1996?

30. Hockey
Who scored eight goals in helping Britain win the Olympic men's gold medal in 1988?

31. Tennis
Who was the last man to defeat Pete Sampras in the Wimbledon singles in the 1990s?

32. Football
Which British international won his 119th and last cap during the 1986 World Cup finals?

33. Football
Who was in Scotland's World Cup squad in 1982 and also helped his country to qualify for France 98?

34. Golf
Which South African won the US Open in 1965, the first non-American champion since 1920?

35. Tennis
Who was the unseeded American who was defeated in the 1996 Wimbledon men's single final?

36. Snooker
Who was the first player to make a 147 at the Crucible in the World Championships?

37. Football
With which club did Peter Shilton make his 1,000th league appearance?

38. Athletics
Britain's Mary Rand and Lyn Davies both won Olympic golds in 1964, but in which event?

39. Boxing
Which former triple world champion won his 100th professional title fight in 1999?

40. Horse Racing
Who was National Hunt champion jockey seven times from 1975 to 1985?

41. Rugby League
Which was the last club to win successive Challenge Cup Finals at Wembley in the twentieth century?

42. Golf
Which American defeated Costantino Rocca to win the 1995 Open after a play-off?

43. Boxing
Which boxer was famously known as the Hitman?

44. Rugby Union
Who scored the late try for Wales which stopped England winning the Grand Slam in 1999?

45. Cricket
Name the player who has taken the most Test wickets for England.

46. Snooker
Who at 23 years and 1 month became the youngest world champion in 1972?

47. Rugby Union
At the 1999 World Cup Neil Jenkins broke whose record for the most individual points in internationals?

48. Motor Racing
Which underdog was a popular winner of the European Grand Prix at the Nurburgring in 1999?

49. Motor Cycling
Who in 1999 won his fourth World Superbike Championship?

50. General
In which sport was Andy Hicks a semi-finalist at the 1995 World Championships?

51. Olympics
In which sport did David Starbrook win an Olympic silver medal in 1972 and a bronze in 1976?

52. Swimming
Who was Britain's only female gold medallist at the 1999 European Championships?

53. Rugby Union
Name the brothers who played for the All Blacks in the 1995 World Cup Final?

54. Darts
Who lost in five World Professional finals between 1978 and 1988?

55. Swimming
Which man won a record nine Olympic titles from 1968 to 1972?

56. Hockey
Nicknamed Jasper, she's Britain's record goalscorer – who is she?

57. General
Which race did Stephen Roche of Ireland win in 1987?

58. American Football
Which team lost four successive Super Bowls from 1991 to 1994?

59. Basketball
Michael Jordan won six NBA championships with which team?

60. Motor Racing
Which is the slowest track on the Grand Prix circuit?

Pink

1. Football
Who was the first player to be sent off in a League Cup Final at Wembley?

2. Boxing
Who was Britain's last Olympic champion before 2000?

3. Snooker
Which ranking title did John Parrott win in Deauville in 1989 and Lyon in 1990?

4. General Sport
What disappeared from Westminster Hall in 1966?

5. Football
Which current Everton player, like his father, has played for Scotland?

6. Cricket
Which bowler twice took over 40 wickets in an Ashes series in the 1980s?

7. Motor Racing
Who was the first man to win the world title driving a car bearing his own name?

8. General
Which annual competition takes place on the grounds of Beaufort Hotel in Gloucestershire?

9. Football
Who left Arsenal in 1980 and played for four Italian clubs?

10. Cricket
Which former England captain's brother Steve played in an FA Cup Final in the 1980s?

11. Boxing
Who was the referee of the Bugner-Cooper clash of 1971 who sadly died in 1999?

12. Swimming
Which British swimmer won a breaststroke gold medal at the 1980 Olympics?

13. Golf
Magnolia, Flowering Peach and Carolina Cherry are holes at which famous course?

14. Football
In 1981 Everton knocked which club out of the FA Cup, so preventing them from appearing in four successive finals?

15. Boxing
Which legendary fighter once defended his world heavyweight title on a record 25 occasions?

16. Rugby Union
Which forward led England to the Grand Slam in 1980 and also captained the British Lions?

17. Darts
Which world champion once won £102,000 for

scoring the first 501 with the minimum nine darts in a major event?

18. Football
Who was the only Englishman to score three or more goals in an international in the 1970s?

19. Motor Racing
Name either of the Scots who won the world title prior to 2000?

20. General
Which sport forbids any competitor to play left-handed?

21. Cricket
Which South African player in 2000 has a father and an uncle who also played Test cricket?

22. Boxing
Henry Cooper and Muhammad Ali contested a world title fight on which league football ground?

23. Football
Name the two Portuguese sides who've won the European Cup.

24. Tennis
Which British woman won the French singles title in 1976?

25. Horse Racing
Name the winning horse in the 1991 Grand National that shared its name with the sponsor of the race?

26. Cricket
Who was the first West Indian bowler to take 400 Test wickets?

27. Baseball
Name the two players who in 1998 beat Roger Maris' 37-year-old record of 61 home runs in a season?

28. Golf
Tony Jacklin won the Open in 1969 – who was the next Briton to win the title?

29. Tennis
Which man in 1995 appeared in his seventh Wimbledon final?

30. Swimming
Who won the gold medal for Britain in the 200 metres breaststroke at the 1976 Olympics?

31. Football
Name the two clubs who met in the last all-London FA Cup final of the twentieth century.

32. Boxing
Who was known as the Clones Cyclone?

33. General
With which sport do you associate the Hawaii Ironman?

34. Cricket
Who in 1977 became the first batsman to score his 100th first-class century in a Test match?

35. Horse Racing
On which course is the Kentucky Derby run annually?

36. Golf
Which player has won a record six US Masters titles?

37. Rugby Union
Who was the legendary Irishman who led the British Lions in 1974?

38. Rugby League
Which current player appeared in Challenge Cup Finals for Wigan, Widnes and St Helens in the 1990s?

39. Snooker
Which player in the 1998 World Championship recorded a record 14 century breaks?

40. Football
Who was the first British manager to win the European Cup three times?

41. Horse Racing
Which 100-1 shot beat Desert Orchid in the 1990 Cheltenham Gold Cup?

42. Tennis
Who was the French woman who reached the Wimbledon singles final for the first time in 1998 at her 14th attempt?

43. Rugby League
Who is the only player to score four tries in a Challenge Cup Final?

44. American Football
Quarterback John Elway helped which side to win the Super Bowl in 1998?

45. Basketball
Who scored over 38,000 points from 1970 to 1989 for the Lakers and Milwaukee Bucks?

46. Baseball
Why was there no winner of the World Series in 1994?

47. General
Who in 1990 was voted the BBC Sports Personality of the Year, the first footballer since Bobby Moore in 1966 to win the award?

48. Athletics
Which charismatic figure lost his world triple jump record to Jonathan Edwards in 1995?

49. General
Which annual event first staged in 1981 had joint winners in Dick Beardsley and Inge Simonsen?

50. Football
Which club won the only all-London FA Cup Final of the 1970s?

1. Football
Which player won League Championship medals with Liverpool and Nottingham Forest?

2. Golf
On which Merseyside course did Roberto de Vicenzo win his Open title in 1967?

3. Snooker
Who was the first Englishman to win the world title at the Crucible?

4. Boxing
Who was Muhammad Ali's famous trainer?

5. Football
Who was the last man to captain the FA Cup winners in successive years prior to 2000?

6. Olympics
In which sport did Briton Max Sciandri win bronze medal in 1996?

7. Cricket
Who captained England when they regained the Ashes in 1970-1?

8. General
With which sport do you associate Mike Hailwood, a former world champion?

9. Football
Who is the only player to score in the final of the FA Cup and European Cup?

10. Rugby League
Which legendary player has captained St Helens, Warrington and Leigh to Challenge Cup wins?

11. Cricket
On the day Graham Gooch retired, which Worcestershire batsman scored his 94th first-class hundred against Essex?

12. Cricket
Which Englishman has played in three World Cup Finals?

13. Horse Racing
Which trainer's last Grand National runner was Nathan Lad before retiring from the sport in 1999?

14. Football
Which was the first London club to win the League Cup?

15. Athletics
Complete this Olympic gold medal-winning quartet – Esmie, Gilbert, Surin and . . .?

16. Golf
Two Australians won the Open in the 1990s – Greg Norman and who else?

17. Boxing
Who is the only man to win three Lonsdale Belts outright?

18. Tennis
Which woman has won the most Wimbledon titles in total in the singles and doubles events?

19. Football
England failed to qualify for the 1974 World Cup when they failed to beat which side in their final qualifying match?

20. Rugby Union
Who was the last Welshman to captain a British Lions touring side?

21. Football
Who played for Blackburn, Newcastle and Leeds in the European Cup in the 1990s?

22. Football
How did Laurent Blanc's goal against Paraguay in France 1998 make World Cup history?

23. Olympics
In which year were the Olympic Games last held in Britain?

24. General
In which sport did Stephen Cousins win eight National Titles by 1998 and finish sixth in the 1998 Winter Olympics?

25. Horse Racing
Who was the last amateur jockey to win the Grand National?

26. Tennis
Which player was defeated in three Wimbledon

men's singles finals in the 1990s?

27. Wrestling
What are the two styles of wrestling recognised in international competition?

28. Athletics
Which American twice broke the world 100 metres record in the 1990s, but never won a major title?

29. Football
Name the two Welshmen who cored in the final of the European Cup Winners Cup in the 1990s.

30. Cricket
Which Englishman in the 1990s scored 6,407 Test runs, the most by any player in the decade?

31. Boxing
Who held the world heavyweight title for 11 years 25 days?

32. Golf
Who made his Ryder Cup debut in 1977 and played in 11 successive competitions?

33. Football
Which club recorded the biggest win of the Premiership in 1999-2000 when they defeated Sheffield Wednesday 8-0?

34. Equestrianism
On which horse did Princess Anne win the European Three-Day Event Championship in 1971?

35. Cricket
Which was the last county, prior to 2000, to win successive Country Championships?

36. Snooker
Who did Steve Davis defeat to win his first world title?

37. Football
Which player in 1991 and 1998 finished on the losing side in the FA Cup Final with different clubs?

38. Boxing
Which Briton won a world title in 1974 beating Jorge Ahumada?

39. Tennis
Who was the Frenchman who reached a Grand Slam singles final in 1997?

40. Golf
Which British golfer played in his eighth Ryder Cup in 1997, without winning a singles match?

41. Football
Who managed the winning FA Cup finalists in 1970 and the losing finalists in 1979, with different clubs?

42. General
By what name is Jennifer Susan Harvey, one of the most respected figures in her sport, better known?

43. Cricket
Which Australian fast bowler took a record 41 wickets in Australia in 1978-9 in the Ashes series?

44. Motor Racing
Which Far Eastern country hosted its first Grand Prix in 1999?

45. General
In which sport did Richard Burns win a World Championship event in 1998?

46. Football
Between 1988 and 2000 there was only one FA Cup Final-winning captain who failed to gain a full international cap in his career – who was he?

47. Snooker
In which country did John Parrott win a tournament in 1998-9?

48. Boxing
Which Britain boxer lost world title fights to Nigel Benn, Chris Eubank and Robin Reid?

Answers

Red

1.	Middlesbrough	**43.**	Michael Owen
2.	Sheffield	**44.**	Boxing
3.	Six	**45.**	Nottinghamshire
4.	Mark Hughes	**46.**	Eric Bristow
5.	Eleven	**47.**	Nicolas Anelka, Eric Cantona
6.	Steve Davis	**48.**	Michael Johnson
7.	Ally McCoist	**49.**	47 minutes
8.	Australia	**50.**	Jimmy White
9.	Aintree	**51.**	Derby County, Darlington
10.	100 metres	**52.**	Bradford
11.	Lawn tennis	**53.**	400 metres hurdles
12.	Bolton	**54.**	New Zealand
13.	Australia	**55.**	US Masters
14.	Colin Jackson	**56.**	Kriss Akabussi
15.	Steve Ogrizovic	**57.**	Dan Petrescu
16.	Silverstone	**58.**	Shaquille O'Neal
17.	Italy	**59.**	Martina Hingis
18.	Robbie and Henry Paul	**60.**	English
19.	Vijay Singh	**61.**	Kieren Fallon
20.	Emile Heskey	**62.**	Orange
21.	Matt Elliott	**63.**	West Indies
22.	Stephen Hendry	**64.**	Michael Atherton
23.	Pete Sampras	**65.**	LA Lakers
24.	Canada	**66.**	Every four years
25.	Rivaldo	**67.**	Seven
26.	Epsom	**68.**	72
27.	Triple jump	**69.**	Will Carling
28.	Mika Hakkinen	**70.**	Two
29.	Australia	**71.**	Mark James
30.	St Helens	**72.**	Sally Gunnell
31.	Paul Lawrie	**73.**	Robbie Fowler
32.	Jenny Pitman	**74.**	Wing
33.	Jacques Villeneuve	**75.**	Chicago Bulls
34.	Richard Gough	**76.**	Conchita Martinez
35.	South Africa	**77.**	Claudio Taffarel
36.	Wigan	**78.**	As referees
37.	Tiger Woods	**79.**	France
38.	Scotland	**80.**	London Broncos
39.	Swedish	**81.**	Kenny Dalglish
40.	Colin Jackson	**82.**	Triple jump
41.	Mark Williams		
42.	Pat Cash		

83. Jack Nicklaus
84. Five
85. Basketball
86. Finnish
87. Australia
88. Craig Stadler
89. 100 metres
90. Crystal Palace
91. Jason Robinson
92. LA Lakers
93. French Open
94. Alan Shearer
95. John Parrott
96. Lester Piggott
97. Two
98. Quinton Fortune
99. Long Jump
100. Tiger Woods
101. Magic Johnson
102. Silverstone
103. Prop
104. St Andrews
105. Namibian
106. Brazil
107. Halifax
108. Flushing Meadow, New York
109. Joe Johnson
110. The Oaks
111. Nicolas Anelka
112. Seb Coe
113. Nigel Mansell
114. Five
115. The Springboks
116. Germany
117. Rugby Union
118. American
119. Venus and Serena Williams
120. Stephen Hendry
121. Dennis Rodman
122. British Lions
123. Australian
124. Denise Lewis
125. Liverpool
126. Bradford Northern
127. Daley Thompson
128. Jose Maria Olazabal

129. End of the match
130. Murrayfield
131. Sergei Bubka
132. Eighteen
133. Iestyn Harris
134. American football
135. Golf
136. Virginia Wade
137. Greg and Jonny Searle
138. Didier Deschamps
139. Swimming
140. Murrayfield
141. Wayne Gretzky
142. Jesse Owens
143. Will Carling
144. Ray Reardon
145. Andre Agassi
146. Gianfranco Zola
147. Aston Villa
148. Muhammad Ali
149. Underwood
150. Wigan
151. Mark Bright (Crystal Palace and Sheffield Wednesday)
152. Fifteen
153. David Lloyd
154. Three-year-olds
155. Four
156. USA
157. Manchester
158. Ian Rush
159. Brian Lara
160. Joe Bugner
161. Eight
162. Black
163. Longchamps
164. Canada
165. Mike Tyson
166. Pakistan
167. Italy
168. Australia
169. 1987
170. Trevor Francis
171. There isn't one
172. The Boat Race
173. The Refrigerator
174. West Ham Utd

175. Dickie Bird
176. Benetton
177. Richard Dunwoody
178. Germany
179. Edgbaston
180. Michael Owen
181. James 'Buster' Douglas
182. Matthew Pinsent
183. Basketball
184. Seven
185. Seve Ballesteros
186. Bryan Robson
187. Three
188. Rio Ferdinand
189. Jane Couch
190. Jensen
191. Greg Chappell
192. Ben Johnson
193. Marseille
194. Sir Richard Hadlee
195. Australia
196. Fore
197. Newmarket
198. Super-heavyweight
199. Shane Warne
200. Rowing
201. Ice Skating
202. Arsene Wenger
203. Heavyweight
204. Lord's
205. Ten
206. Henry Cecil
207. Michael Schumacher
208. Joe Bugner
209. Ivan Lendl
210. Ten
211. Mike Gatting
212. Darts
213. Tennis
214. Neville Southall
215. Houston
216. Jackie Stewart
217. Phil de Glanville
218. Graham Taylor
219. Boxing
220. Germany
221. Riddick Bowe

222. West Ham United
223. Tobogganing
224. Jenson Button
225. Warwickshire
226. Kevin Keegan
227. Squash
228. Istabraq
229. Arsene Wenger
230. Sunderland
231. Athletics (shot putt)
232. Aston Villa
233. USA
234. Lester Piggott
235. Linford Christie
236. Nigel Mansell
237. Borussia Dortmund
238. St Louis Rams
239. Martin Johnson
240. Monica Seles
241. George Foreman
242. Denmark
243. Badminton
244. Tony Cascarino
245. Mark Williams
246. Frankie Dettori
247. Gianfranco Zola
248. Tour de France
249. Judo
250. Andy Linighan
251. Ayrton Senna
252. Mike Catt
253. Martin Offiah
254. Hamburg
255. Tour de France
256. Michael Stich
257. Welterweight
258. Joe Royle, Terry Venables
259. Football (the World Cup)
260. Jenny and Mark Pitman
261. Stirling Moss
262. Neil Jenkins
263. Greg Rusedski
264. Lennox Lewis
265. Hampshire
266. Gordon Strachan

267. Tour de France
268. Jayne Torvill and Christopher Dean
269. Walter Swinburn
270. Ivan Lendl
271. Newcastle United
272. Terry Griffiths
273. Darts
274. Grand National
275. Newcastle United
276. Long jump
277. Indianapolis
278. Australia
279. Robbie Paul
280. Denver Broncos
281. Show Jumping Derby
282. Tottenham Hotspur
283. Darts
284. Ice Hockey
285. David Platt
286. Australia
287. Seattle
288. Rigobert Song
289. Graham and Damon Hill
290. Ally McCoist
291. Epsom
292. Will Carling
293. Andre Agassi
294. Herbie Hide
295. Kenny Dalglish
296. Barnum
297. Nigel Mansell
298. Glamorgan
299. John Lowe
300. Lazio

Yellow

1. Marc Overmars
2. Javelin
3. Seoul
4. Alex Ferguson
5. Rugby Union
6. Courtney Walsh
7. Graeme Le Saux and Matt Le Tissier
8. Naseem Hamed
9. Cheltenham
10. Paul Scholes
11. Marco Fu
12. Martin Pipe
13. Nottingham Forest
14. David Coulthard
15. Jonny Wilkinson
16. Wigan
17. Don Hutchison
18. Nasser Hussain
19. Mike Tyson
20. Darlington
21. Czech Republic
22. Colin Montgomerie
23. Cassius Clay (Muhammad Ali)
24. Rallying
25. Oliver Bierhoff
26. Greg Rusedski
27. Alex Higgins
28. James Hunt
29. Sally Gunnell
30. Les and Rio Ferdinand
31. Iuean Evans
32. Frank Sinclair
33. West Indies
34. Frank Bruno
35. Red Rum
36. High jump
37. Roberton Baggio
38. Ian Baker-Finch
39. Williams
40. Lothar Matthaus
41. Flo Jo
42. Bjorn Borg
43. Zinedine Zidane
44. France
45. Steve Robinson
46. 147
47. The Oval
48. Kenny Daglish
49. Lester Piggott
50. Jonny Wilkinson
51. John Daly
52. Terry Venables, Bobby Robson
53. Denver Broncos

54. Breaststroke
55. Laura Davies
56. Gabriel Batistuta
57. Bradford Bulls, Leeds Rhinos
58. Allan Border
59. Centre
60. Long jump
61. Pat Rafter
62. Arnold Muhren
63. International Olympic Committee
64. The Nevilles
65. LA Lakers
66. Alan Shearer
67. New Zealand
68. Suny Bay
69. Steve Davis
70. Michael Schumacher

Green

1. Martin Johnson
2. Sheffield Wednesday
3. Steve Davis
4. Lord Gyllene
5. Bob Anderson
6. Peter Schmeichel
7. Graham Gooch
8. Allan Wells
9. Martin Offiah
10. Nigeria
11. Jeremy Guscott
12. John Curry, Robin Cousins
13. Cameroon
14. Steve Collins
15. Eddie Irvine
16. Sergio Garcia
17. Andreas Brehme
18. AC Milan
19. Steve Waugh
20. Freddie Starr
21. Barry Sheene
22. Nick Faldo
23. Howard Wilkinson
24. Nashwan

25. 23
26. Warrington
27. Liverpool
28. Edinburgh
29. Speedway
30. Dalton Grant
31. Graham Gooch
32. John Leslie
33. Jack Charlton
34. The Curragh
35. Sheffield Eagles
36. Ernie Els
37. Baseball
38. Dave Beasant
39. Oliver McCall
40. Steffi Graf
41. Rowing
42. Athletics
43. Gary Lineker
44. Ron Atkinson
45. Steve Redgrave
46. Liz McColgan
47. Frank Bruno
48. Jonathan Davies
49. Nayim
50. Valderrama
51. Motor cycling
52. Los Angeles
53. Lester Piggott
54. Bobby Charlton
55. Cameroon
56. Ben Cohen
57. Ken Doherty
58. Tom Watson
59. Japan
60. Water skiing
61. Colin McRae
62. Curtis Strange
63. Nijinsky
64. Most Valuable Player
65. Kelly Holmes
66. Allan Donald
67. Tottenham Hotspur
68. Mike Denness
69. Jackie Stewart
70. Cassius Clay

Brown

1. John Harkes
2. Jimmy White
3. Miguel Indurain
4. Mario Kempes
5. Clive Lloyd
6. Carl Llewellyn
7. Seb Coe
8. Kevin Richardson
9. Mike Tyson
10. Kapil Dev
11. Richard Krajicek
12. Italy
13. Ken Doherty
14. Brazil
15. Yachting
16. Super middleweight
17. Jenny Pitman
18. John Collins
19. Shane Warne
20. Seb Coe
21. Eric Cantona
22. Dunga
23. Carl Lewis
24. Richard Hadlee
25. Marathon
26. Olivier Peslier
27. Dennis Taylor
28. Alan Shearer
29. Iwan Thomas
30. Justin Rose (because he was an amateur)
31. Jana Novotna
32. Wim Jansen (Celtic)
33. Barnsley
34. The Belfry
35. Steve Cauthen
36. Nine
37. Michel Platini
38. Jo Durie
39. Darts
40. Larry Holmes
41. Bob Taylor
42. Olga Korbut
43. Brian Fletcher
44. Jamie Carragher
45. Fencing
46. Wayne McCullough
47. Mary Peters
48. Sandy Lyle
49. Cycling
50. Dennis Bergkamp
51. Angus Fraser
52. Darts
53. Steffi Graf
54. Spain
55. Graeme Hick
56. Lothar Matthaus
57. Jack Nicklaus
58. Loftus Road (QPR)
59. Dennis Rodman
60. Ryder Cup

Blue

1. Toto Schillaci
2. Pietro Mennea
3. Bob Massie
4. Scunthorpe United
5. Peter Fleming
6. John Conteh
7. Lee Dixon
8. Mark Pitman
9. Paul Lawrie
10. Ray Wilkins
11. Costa Rica
12. Bob Champion
13. Daley Thompson
14. Ipswich Town, Tottenham Hotspur
15. Alain Prost
16. Newcastle
17. Shaun Edwards
18. Mark Taylor
19. Roma
20. Ice Hockey
21. Ronald and Erwin Koeman
22. Warrington
23. Denis Andries
24. Ice Skating
25. Ilie Nastase
26. Ally McLeod
27. South African

28.	Cycling	**9.**	Liam Brady
29.	Tony Allcock	**10.**	Mike Gatting
30.	Sean Kerly	**11.**	Harry Gibbs
31.	Richard Krajicek	**12.**	Duncan Goodhew
32.	Pat Jennings	**13.**	Augusta
33.	Jim Leighton	**14.**	Arsenal
34.	Gary Player	**15.**	Joe Louis
35.	Mal Washington	**16.**	Bill Beaumont
36.	Cliff Thorburn	**17.**	John Lowe
37.	Leyton Orient	**18.**	Malcolm Macdonald
38.	Long jump	**19.**	Jackie Stewart, Jim Clark
39.	Julio Cesar Chavez		
40.	John Francome	**20.**	Polo
41.	St Helens	**21.**	Shaun Pollock
42.	John Daly	**22.**	Highbury
43.	Thomas Hearns	**23.**	Benfica and Porto
44.	Scott Gibbs	**24.**	Sue Barker
45.	Ian Botham	**25.**	Seagram
46.	Alex Higgins	**26.**	Courtney Walsh
47.	Michael Lynagh	**27.**	Mark McGwire and Sammy Sosa
48.	Johnny Herbert		
49.	Carl Fogarty	**28.**	Sandy Lyle
50.	Snooker	**29.**	Boris Becker
51.	Judo	**30.**	David Wilkie
52.	Sue Rolph	**31.**	Tottenham and QPR
53.	Zinzan and Robin Brooke	**32.**	Barry McGuigan
		33.	Triathlon
54.	John Lowe	**34.**	Geoff Boycott
55.	Mark Spitz	**35.**	Churchill Downs
56.	Jane Sixsmith	**36.**	Jack Nicklaus
57.	Tour de France	**37.**	Willie John McBride
58.	Buffalo Bills	**38.**	Bobbie Goulding
59.	Chicago Bulls	**39.**	John Higgins
60.	Monaco	**40.**	Bob Paisley
		41.	Norton's Coin
		42.	Nathalie Tauziat
		43.	Leroy Rivett

Pink

		44.	Denver Broncos
		45.	Kareen Abdul-Jabbar
1.	Andrei Kanchelskis	**46.**	There was a players' strike
2.	Chris Finnegan		
3.	European Open	**47.**	Paul Gascoigne
4.	The World Cup football trophy	**48.**	Willie Banks
		49.	London Marathon
5.	Scott Gemmill	**50.**	West Ham United
6.	Terry Alderman		
7.	Jack Brabham		
8.	Badminton Horse Trials		

Black

1. Larry Lloyd
2. Hoylake
3. John Spencer
4. Angelo Dundee
5. Steven Perryman
6. Cycling
7. Ray Illingworth
8. Motor Cycling
9. Teddy Sheringham
10. Alex Murphy
11. Graeme Hick
12. Graham Gooch
13. Jenny Pitman
14. Chelsea
15. Donovan Bailey
16. Ian Baker-Finch
17. Henry Cooper
18. Billie Jean King
19. Poland
20. Phil Bennett
21. David Batty
22. It was the first World Cup Golden Goal decider
23. 1948
24. Ice Skating
25. Marcus Armytage
26. Goran Ivanisevic
27. Freestyle and Greco-Roman
28. Leroy Burrell
29. Mark Hughes (Manchester United) and John Hartson (Arsenal)
30. Alec Stewart
31. Joe Louis
32. Nick Faldo
33. Newcastle United
34. Doublet
35. Warwickshire
36. Doug Mountjoy
37. Steve Pearce
38. John Conteh
39. Cedric Pioline
40. Ian Woosnam
41. Dave Sexton
42. Jenny Pitman
43. Rodney Hogg
44. Malaysia
45. Rallying
46. Steve Bruce
47. Germany (Masters)
48. Henry Wharton

The Trivia Challenge

The Trivia Challenge comprises 12 formulaic quizzes, each with three different parts.

The first part, Sporting Mastermind, is a pot-pourri of thought-inducing questions – a combination of quotes, odd men out, naming the year – and the Before You Go question is one which will test even the best of you. The quotes are interesting, of course – I can even remember one attributed to me when I lost the 1989 world final to Steve Davis rather 'heavily'. I said, 'I played like a slow puncture.'

The second part, Sports Days, reminds us of birthdays & anniversaries, month by month, while the third part, Local Heroes has a local theme, moving us around Britain, as well as other topical themes.

Then you'll find the last Trivia Challenge test: 'And Finally'. This is one which the *Question of Sport* lads will enjoy – have a quick look now, but you'll agree they'll take some answering so like me, you'll use them in clubs, pubs, schools or at the match.

Quiz 1
Sporting Mastermind

1. Who Scored the Goal?
'Before the game had gone 60 seconds, the Italian picked up the ball on Wembley's wide open spaces and ran unopposed . . .'

2. Odd Man Out
Which of these countries has yet to win the Cricket World Cup?
a) Australia b) India c) New Zealand d) Pakistan
e) Sri Lanka

3. In Common
What do this trio have in common?
a) John White b) Capt Brown c) Esha Ness

4. Who Said This?
Who in 1998 said after a Premiership derby: 'It's a great satisfaction to see two teams I coached draw 0-0.'

5. Name the Year
a) Aravinda da Silva scored a World Cup Final century
b) Frankie Dettori rode seven winners in a day at cumulative odds of 25,095-1
c) Robbie Paul scored Wembley's first hat-trick of tries in a Challenge Cup Final – but still finished on the losing side.

d) England were defeated in the European Championship finals on penalties.

6. Picture
This outstanding young striker scored 222 goals in six seasons. Who is he and for which Football League team did he play?

7. Think About it
Which current Premiership manager played in an FA Cup Final in the 1970s, 1980s and 1990s?

8. The Name's the Same
Two England centre-halves of the 1980s have the same Christian name and surname – who are they?

9. Before You Go
Up to Euro 2000, name the last 10 players to appear for England in a full international while playing for Newcastle United.

Sports Days

January
1. Who in the 1965 Honours list became the first footballer to receive a knighthood?

2. In the 1989 Honours list, a darts player received an honour for the first time – who was he?

3. 4 January is the birthdate of a former Olympic

boxing champion who was the first man to regain the world heavyweight title in 1960 – who is he?

4. On 6 January 1959 this great all-rounder was born, a cricketer who captained India to victory in the 1983 World Cup – can you name him?

5. On 7 January Abraham Saperstein founded one of the world's best known basketball teams in 1927. They were renowned for their comedy routines and showmanship – but who were they?

6. On 13 January 1969, the youngest world snooker champion was born – name him.

7. On 17 January 1942, the BBC's Sportsman of the Century was born – who is he?

8. Which Briton on 25 January 1992 in New Zealand became the first man to throw the modified javelin 300 feet?

9. Who on 31 January 1965 was appointed manager of Celtic and two years later guided them to the European Cup Final defeat of Inter Milan?

10. Which non-league club knocked Coventry City out of the FA Cup on 7 January 1989?

11. Who won the Wimbledon men's singles in 1988 and 1990 and was born on 19 January 1966 in Sweden?

12. Which famous snooker player recorded the first televised maximum 147 break on 11 January 1982 at Oldham?

13. On 21 January 1940, this American golfer first saw the light of day. His first Major title was won in 1962 (the US Open) and his sixth US Masters title was won in 1986 at the age of 42 – but who is he?

14. Britain's most successful football manager was born on 23 January 1919. He captured six league titles and three European Cups among other titles – can you name him?

15. Which American on 24 January 1999 carded a 59 to equal the lowest ever round on the US PGA tour?

Local Heroes

Firsts

1. General
The Green Bay Packers were the first ever winners of which annual sporting event?

2. Athletics
Who won the first World Championship Decathlon title in 1983?

3. Basketball
Which legendary player in 1962 became the first man to score 100 points in an NBA game?

4. General
Of which coveted world championship was John L Sullivan the first winner in 1882?

5. Cricket
Only two players have scored over 10,000 runs in Test cricket – Allan Border was the second, but which Indian batsman was the first?

6. Football
Who were the first side to win the European Cup
and also the first to win it in the new Millennium?

7. Horse Racing
Which jockey had his first Derby winner in 1954
and his last in 1983?

8. Ice Skating
Who in 1976 became the first British Olympic
men's champion?

9. Football
Name the Ipswich Town player who in 1981
became the first overseas international footballer
to win the Football Writers' Player of the Year?

10. Motor Racing
Who was the first British world champion?

11. Rugby League
Which club in 1999 won their first Grand Final?

12. Rugby Union
Which club in 1997-98 became the first British
club to win the European Cup?

13. Snooker
Who in 1977 was the first Englishman to win the
world title at the Crucible?

14. Tennis
Who was the first Dutchman to win the men's
singles title at Wimbledon?

15. Football
Who was the first Football Writers' Player of the
Year in 1948 and then the first European Player of
the Year in 1956?

Quiz 2
Sporting Mastermind

1. Spot the Incident
'After surviving a second-minute possible caution by referee Roger Milford for laying his boots into Garry Parker, his Cup Final was ended 13 minutes later following a desperate lunge into Gary Charles . . .'

2. Odd Man Out
Which of these Wimbledon champions won the title on more than one occasion?
a) Richard Krajicek b) Andre Agassi c) Michael Stich d) Stefan Edberg e) Pat Cash

3. In Common
Which club comes next in this list – Preston, Aston Villa, Tottenham, Arsenal, Liverpool?

4. Who Said This?
Of which sport did commentator Tony Green famously remark in 1981: 'My word, you need to be fit to play this now!'

5. Name the Year
a) Michael Owen made his England debut
b) Jana Novotna won the Wimbledon singles
c) Mark Foster, James Hickman and Susan Rolph won swimming gold medals at the Commonwealth games.

d) Arsenal reduced Man Utd's Premiership lead
thanks to Marc Overmars' winner at Old Trafford

6. Picture
What was a young Barry
McGuigan celebrating in
1978 in this picture?

7. Think About it
Who between 1984 and
1998 played in FA Cup
Finals with three different
clubs

8. The Name's the Same
a) Grand National winning jockey b) a Scottish rugby
union forward c) Liverpool strongman and former
captain of the 1960s and 70s d) the 1968 Olympic
200 metres champion and Black Power advocate.

9. Before You Go
Up to Euro 2000, six Middlesbrough and five
Sunderland players had played for England in full
internationals while at those clubs. Can you name
them?

Sports Days

February

1. Who on 1 February 1979 became British
football's first £1 million player?

2. Which horse 8 February 1983 was kidnapped
from a stable in Ireland?

3. Which golfer was born on 9 February 1958
and won the British Open in 1985 and the US
Masters in 1988?

4. 14 February 1951 is the birthdate of a current manager who played for Hamburg and Southampton among other clubs – who is he?

5. Who on 14 February 1989 became the third jockey to ride 1,000 National Hunt winners?

6. Which current Premiership manager (as at July 2000) was born on 18 February 1933?

7. Who on 22 February 1991 shocked football, after his side had drawn 4-4 in an FA Cup game, by quitting as manager of a top English club?

8. Who on 25 February 1964 won the world heavyweight title in Florida by beating Sonny Liston?

9. Which famous race was run for the first time on 26 February 1839, won by Lottery and ridden by Jem Mason?

10. Which Australian on 26 February 1993 became the most prolific scorer in Test cricket?

11. Who was the Clones Cyclone born on 28 February 1961, who won the world featherweight title in 1985 beating Eusebio Pedroza?

12. Which famous footballer signed for Leeds 'on loan' on 2 February 1992 after walking out on Sheffield Wednesday?

13. Who on 10 February 1999 scored both France's goals at Wembley, their first win at the stadium in a full international?

14. On 5 February 1992 which club became the first from the top flight to lose an FA Cup game on penalties when losing out to Southampton?

15. Which British woman broke the world indoor triple jump record to win gold at the World Championships in Valencia on 28 February 1998?

Local Heroes

Midlands Sport

1. Football
Which was the last non-league club to knock out a top-flight club from the FA Cup?

2. Athletics
Who was the only Briton to win an Olympic javelin gold medal in the twentieth century?

3. Cricket
Which Englishman took a Test hat-trick in 1995?

4. Football
Who at the age of 16 scored 15 goals in his first 15 games in the old Second Division and managed the same club in 1999-2000?

5. Rugby Union
Which Nottingham-born 'Pit Bull' made 64 appearances for England in the hooking position from 1987 to 1995?

6. Football
Only two Midlands sides won the FA Cup from 1965 to 2000 – who were they?

7. General
With which sport do you associate William Henry Hare?

8. Boxing
Which Telford boxer lost his WBC world super-middleweight title to Marcus Beyer in 1999?

9. Football
Which club did Aston Villa defeat to win the European Cup?

10. Snooker
Who was born in Derbyshire in 1913 and won his first ranking points at the 1974 World Championships?

11. Football
Who played for West Bromwich Albion and Wolves and scored on his debut for England against Scotland while in the old Third Division in 1989?

12. Football
Who managed Aston Villa when they won the European Cup in 1982?

13. Rugby Union
Which Leicester forward captained the Lions on their last trip to South Africa?

14. Boxing
Which Warley fighter won an Olympic medal in 1976 and lost a world title fight in round one to Azumah Nelson?

15. Cricket
Name the Hong Kong-born player who won the Man of the Match award in the NatWest Final with Sussex and Warwickshire and played for England?

Quiz 3
Sporting Mastermind

1) Who Am I?

1. I was born in 1964 and made my Welsh debut in 1987.

2. I won the Welsh Cup with Llanelli and have captained Wales on many occasions.

3. I joined Bath late in my career and continued to play on the wing.

2) Name the Venues
Which three venues have hosted the British Grand Prix since 1950?

3) Name the Incident
'With 250 yards to go, the 25-year-old student surged into the lead and as he entered the final 40 yards he summoned up all his strength to break that impossible barrier . . .'

4) Who Said This?
Which TV commentator once said: 'Don't tell those coming in the final result of this fantastic match, but let's just have another look at Italy's winning goal'?

5) Think About it
What record did Ryan Green take from Ryan Giggs in 1998?

6) Olympic Hero
Why is Edward Eagan unique among all male Olympic gold medal winners?

7) Name the Year
1. Mike Tyson beat Tony Tucker to become undisputed world heavyweight champion.

2. Pat Cash won his only Wimbledon singles title.

3. Tottenham were beaten for the first time in a Wembley FA Cup Final.

8) The Name's the Same
One was a famous England rugby union footballer, the other a famous football commentator.

9) Which Sport?
Which sport is played on a grass lawn 35 yards long by 28 yards wide, with six hoops, a ball, a peg and a mallet?

10) Picture
A fromer captain of England in 1921 and grandson of a famous poet. Who is this cricketing legend?

11) Before You Go
Name the last 10 footballers to appear in a full international for England while playing for a foreign club (non-British).

Sports Days

March

1. Name the West Indian who on 1 March 1958 scored a then world record 365 against Pakistan, a total later exceeded by Brian Lara?

2. Also on 1 March, but in 1980, who died after watching his beloved Everton lose 2-1 in the Merseyside derby – a player generally regarded as the greatest centre-forward of all time due to 60 league goals in one season for the Blues?

3. 4 March 1951 is the birthdate of a player who is still the only Scotsman to win 100 caps for his country – who is he?

4. Who 7 March 1991 captured the British and European heavyweight titles by stopping defending champion Gary Mason at Wembley?

5. Which Ukrainian on 15 March 1991 at an indoor meeting in Spain became the first man to clear 20 ft in a pole vault competition?

6. Which trainer saddled the first five horses past the post in the Cheltenham Gold Cup run in 1983 on 17 March?

7. Two Irishmen share the same birthdate, 18 March. One was the world snooker champion in 1972 and 1982, the other a jockey who won the flat racing championship eleven times from 1974 – but who are they?

8. Who was the Brazilian born on 21 March 1960 who was motor racing world champion in 1988, 1990 and 1991?

9. A winner of four Olympic gold medals in the 1936 Olympics, this great American athlete died on 31 March 1980. Can you name him?

10. On 1 March 1985 this Wigan player played for England aged only 17 and in 2000 he finally retired from rugby league after winning more medals than anyone – who is he?

11. Who on 8 March 1971 gave Muhammad Ali his first professional defeat, although Ali would later gain revenge?

12. Which Orrell player scored three tries for England against Scotland on 15 March 1980?

13. Which pair recorded 29 maximum sixes in the 1984 World Ice Dancing Championships on 22-24 March 1984 in Ottowa, a new world record?

14. Who on 5 March 1999 became the only third man to take 400 Test match wickets?

15. Which athlete broke the indoor 800 metres record on 7 March 1997?

Local Heroes

London Sport

1. Football
Name the two future Chelsea players who played against each other in the 1989 European Cup Final.

2. Rugby Union
Which current England international's middle

names are Bruno Nero?

3. Rugby League
Which club defeated London Broncos 52-16 in the Challenge Cup Final in 1999?

4. Cricket
Who are the Australian-born brothers playing for Surrey who have both played for England?

5. Football
Who scored 414 goals in 591 matches while with three different London clubs?

6. Rugby Union
Which club plays at Old Deer Park?

7. Boxing
Who won his first fight against Lupe Guerra in 1982 and lost his first world heavyweight title challenge in 1986 to Tim Witherspoon?

8. Cricket
Which famous cricketer scored thirteen centuries for Middlesex in 1947 and played for Arsenal in the 1950 FA Cup Final?

9. General
London Towers beat Thames Valley 82-71 in the 1999 Championship Play-Off Final – but in which sport was this?

10. Football
Name the three former England managers who have played for Tottenham.

11. Athletics
Who, within the space of 42 days in July and August 1979, posted new world records over 800 metres, 1500 metres and 1 mile?

12. Football
Who received a yellow card for Chelsea against his former club Sheffield United in a 1992 FA Cup game after just three seconds?

13. General
In which sport did the BDO champion Raymond Van Barneveld lose to the PDC champion Phil Taylor at Wembley in November 1999?

14. Boxing
Which London-born heavyweight lost in a WBC title fight to Lennox Lewis in July 1997, having previously vacated the WBO title?

15. Rugby League
Name the two former Wigan legends who appeared in the London Broncos side which lost the 1999 Challenge Cup Final?

Quiz 4
Sporting Mastermind

1. Name the Year
Liverpool won the League, Man United the FA Cup, Nick Faldo the Open and Mr Frisk the Grand National?

2. Who Scored the Goal?
'The winning goal was the stuff of legends. Replacing Flo, he seized on a superbly chipped pass by Wise and with only his third touch of the ball . . .'

3. In Common
In the FA Cup, what have Sunderland (1991) QPR (1982) West Ham Utd (1980) Southampton (1976) and Fulham (1975) all got in common?

4. Think About it
What makes Ken Norton unique among world heavyweight champions?

5. Odd Man Out
Which is the odd man out in this list of League managers? Ian McFaul, Don Mackay, Mike Walker, Joe Royle and Peter Shilton.

6. Picture
Name the two famous sports stars that appear in this composite picture.

7. The 'O's
Name the six players who appeared in FA Cup Finals in the 1990s whose surnames end in the letter 'O'?

8. Who Am I?
1) I was born in 1957 and I have won six world titles
2) I enjoy soul music and chess
3) One of my books was How To Be Really Interesting

9. Triathlon
What are the three disciplines of the triathlon and over what distances are they contested?

10. The Name's the Same
a) One played at full-back for Liverpool and England
b) The other was a Welsh rugby union half-back?

11. Before You Go
Name the last 15 footballers to appear in a full international for England since 1970 while playing for Manchester City.

Sports Days

April

1. Which horse on 2 April 1977 won his third Grand National at Aintree?

2. An old friend of mine was born on 3 April 1946. His only title was the 1979 UK Championship, but he's now seen mainly on Big Break and as a commentator – who is this 'mimic'?

3. On 4 April of which year did Bob Champion win the Grand National on Aldaniti, just two years after been diagnosed as having cancer?

4. What event got underway on 6 April 1896, the brainchild of Baron Pierre de Coubertin, which has remained with us into the 21st century?

5. Who at the age of 23 years and 4 days became the youngest winner of the US Masters on 13 April 1980?

6. Which club ended Arsenal's dreams of a Cup and League double on 14 April 1991 when winning the first FA Cup semi-final to be played at Wembley?

7. Name the player who on 20 April 1981 won the first of his world titles at the Crucible?

8. After 49 unbeaten fights, which great heavyweight boxer retired from the sport as reigning world champion on 27 April 1956?

9. On 28 April 1990, which Wigan scrum half won his second Lance Todd Trophy as man of the match in the Rugby League Challenge Final?

10. Which club on 29 April 1970 won the FA Cup Final replay at Old Trafford?

11. 13 April 1986 was an unlucky day for which

British driver when he lost the Spanish Grand Prix by just 0.014 seconds to Ayrton Senna?

12. Who did Stephen Hendry defeat on 29 April 1990 to become the youngest snooker world champion?

13. On 5 April 1998, who became the first British squash player to win the British Open in 25 years?

14. Probably the greatest ice hockey player of all time announced his retirement on 16 April 1999 – who was he?

15. Which superstar won the 1997 US Masters by a record twelve shots on 13 April?

Local Heroes

North-East Sport

1. Football
Who played for Sunderland in their famous 1973 FA Cup Final win and went on to play for England with four other clubs?

2. Boxing
Who in June 1989 won the world IBF cruiserweight title, outpointing Patrick Lamumba in Stanley, County Durham?

3. Cricket
Which player has scored the most runs in a county game against Durham?

4. Athletics
Which famous athlete won Britain's only Olympic medal in 1976?

5. Football
Which manager came to the fore in 1974 when winning the Manager of the Year award with Middlesbrough?

6. Rugby Union
Which club won the English clubs Knockout Cup in 1976 and 1977?

7. General
Durham Wasps won the British grand slam of the three main titles in 1990-91, but in which sport?

8. Cricket
Who defeated Durham in the NatWest Trophy third round in 1999?

9. Football
Who scored a hat-trick on his Football League debut against Liverpool in 1996?

10. Rugby League
Who left St Helens and became the coach of Gateshead Thunder in 1998?

11. Swimming
Which British woman won the European 100 metres freestyle title in 1999?

12. Football
Who at the start of the 2000-01 season had scored the most goals in the Premiership?

13. Boxing
Which Sunderland fighter twice lost to Orlando Canizales in world IBF bantamweight title challenges in 1990 and 1991?

14. Rugby Union
Who is the son of a famous cricketing father who joined Newcastle in 2000?

15. Athletics
Which athlete won the first world 1500 metres title in 1983 and is the only Briton to win this title?

Quiz 5
Sporting Mastermind

1. Who Said This?
Who in July 1999 said, 'People will remember it as the one he lost: I have no problems with that – it was his for the taking'?

2. Think About it
When did Rush meet Rush in an FA Cup Final?

3. Who's Missing?
Akabusi, Redmond, Black and . . .?

4. In Common
What have fishing, badminton, ice hockey and two events in athletics, the discus and the hammer, got in common?

5. Name the Incident
'In the 58th minute Pearce clumsily fouled Haessler and although Shilton had Brehme's free kick covered, the ball took a deflection . . .'

6. Heavyweight Heroes
Excluding American-based Michael Bentt, which four British boxers held versions of the world heavyweight title in the 1990s?

7. England's Saints
In March 1981 Southampton fielded five England captains – name them.

8. Name the Year
a) Dennis Taylor won the world title
b) Boris Becker won Wimbledon Singles for the first time
c) Everton won their only European trophy

9. Picture
On which track did this world champion driver die in a fatal crash?

10. Who am I?
a) I was born in 1963 and represented Scotland in the Dunhill Cup
b) I made my Ryder Cup debut in 1991
c) Although I topped the European Order of Merit many times in the 1990s, I did not win a Major in that decade.

11. Before You Go
Since 1980, 16 players have appeared in a full international for England while playing for Aston Villa, up to Euro 2000 – name them.

Sports Days

May

1. Why did a great number of horse racing followers finally have a lot to rejoice about on 1 May 1961?

2. Why did Stanley Matthews and his legion of supporters have a lot to celebrate on 2 May 1953?

3. Which famous race was first run on 4 May 1780 and was won by Diomed?

4. One of the great sporting moments came on 6 May 1954 when which athlete ran a mile in 3 min 59.4 sec?

5. A famous day for one Liverpudlian, 11 May 1964 – but whose birthday is it?

6. This female gymnast won three golds and a silver at the 1972 Olympics, having been born on 16 May 1955 – who is she?

7. Which football club won the European Cup for the fifth consecutive year on 18 May 1960 in Glasgow?

8. Which boxer was defeated by Muhammad Ali at Highbury football stadium on 21 May 1966, the first world heavyweight title contest in London since 1908?

9. Which famous American athlete set a world long jump record on 25 May 1935 which stood until 1960?

10. What annual event took place for the first time on 28 May 1907 on the Isle of Man?

11. What epic achievement was recorded at 11.30am on 29 May 1953 by Sir Edmund Hillary and Sherpa Tenzing?

12. Which West Indian on the last day of May 1984 set a record for the highest score in one-day internationals, scoring 189 not out at Old Trafford?

13. Which club did Ian Rush join on a free transfer on 20 May 1996?

14. Which Worcestershire batsman on 31 May 1998 became the 24th batsman in history to secure 100 hundreds?

15. In which sport did Sweden's Jan-Ove Waldner prevent a Chinese clean sweep at the World Championships on 5 May 1999?

Local Heroes

Merseyside Sport

1. Which player has scored a record five FA Cup final goals at Wembley?

2. Who was the Liverpool boxer who held the world light heavyweight title in the 1970s?

3. Which major race was held on Merseyside on 8 April 2000?

4. Which golf course staged its first Open Championship in 1954 and was the venue for Mark O'Meara's win in 1998?

5. Who played for Everton in 1999-2000 and was the only player to win four FA Cup winners' medals in the last century?

6. Who is the only Liverpudlian to have won the world snooker title?

7. Austin Healey and Paul Grayson, two of

England's rugby union stars, both played for
which Merseyside-based club early in their
careers?

8. Which former Liverpool player was manager
of Wales for 47 days in 1993-94?

9. Which cyclist won an Olympic gold medal in
the 4,000 metres individual pursuit in 1992?

10. Which club defeated Bradford Bulls in the
1996 and 1997 Rugby League Challenge Cup
Finals?

Quiz 6
Sporting Mastermind

1. Who Said This?
Which 'modest' England batsman said in 1974: 'If I'd gone to Cambridge or Oxford, there'd have been no limits to what I could've achieved'?

2. Who Scored the Goal?
'After the penalty, Scotland led 2-1 and soon it was three as . . . scored a great individual effort, beating three players for one of the outstanding goals of the World Cup?'

3. 1966 World Cup
Which three members of England's winning side never played in an FA Cup Final?

4. Who Am I?
a) I was born in the North East in 1960 and set several world records
b) I support Sunderland FC
c) I won a world 1500 metres title but never won an Olympic gold medal?

5. Name the Year
a) Jimmy Connors won Wimbledon eight years after his first win
b) The Commonwealth Games were held in Brisbane

c) Aston Villa won the European Cup

6. In Common
What do England centre Will Greenwood, Test opener Mark Butcher and England striker Nigel Clough all have in common?

7. Strange but True
Which country's goalkeepers in the 1980s had these unusual surnames: Bats, Rust and Dropsy?

8. Think About it
The first all London FA Cup Final in the twentieth century in 1967 and the second in 1975 saw one player appear on both occasions – who was he?

9. Ice Hockey
Where do the following NHL teams come from? a) The Redwings b) The Rangers c) The Oilers

10. The Aussies
Four Australian golfers won the Open Championship in the twentieth century – who are they?

11. Before You Go
Since 1980, six players have appeared for England in full internationals whose surnames end in a double 't' – who are they?

Sports Days

June

1.   Which jockey rode his record ninth Epsom Derby winner, Teenoso, in 1983, on 1 June?

2.   Which famous golfing tournament was inaugurated on 3 June 1927 at Worcester, Massachusetts, with the USA winning 9-2?

3. After 122 successive hurdles victories from 1977 to 1987, which famous American finally lost on 4 June 1987 to Danny Harris?

4. What dubious distinction did Alan Mullery earn in the England v Yugoslavia game in Florence on 5 June 1968?

5. Which player became the youngest winner of a Grand Slam tennis tournament in the twentieth century on 9 June 1990 when winning the French ladies' singles aged 16 years and 6 months?

6. Which Briton set a world record over 800 metres on 10 June 1981 in Florence, which stood throughout the decade?

7. This footballer, born on 12 June 1945, has the distinction of playing for both Arsenal and Tottenham in FA Cup Finals and winning over 100 caps for his country – but who is he?

8. The world's successful motor cyclist was born on 16 June 1943. He won more world titles and races than any other in his career, including world 500cc titles between 1966 and 1975 – but who is he?

9. Which Englishman completed a remarkable Test match against Pakistan on 19 June 1978 when he became the first man to score a century and take eight wickets in an innings in the same Test?

10. Who on 21 June 1970 became the first English golfer since Ted Ray in 1920 to win the US Open?

11. Which country gave England their biggest

defeat ever in rugby union, winning 76-0 on 6 June 1998?

12. Which famous football club won the first European Cup final on 13 June 1956, defeating Rheims 4-3?

13. Who was the Brazilian tennis player who won the French men's singles title on 8 June 1997?

14. Which player on 6 June 1999 became only the fifth man in history to have won all four Grand Slam tennis singles titles?

15. On 20 June 1996 which umpire started his 66th and final Test match, against India at Lord's?

Local Heroes

Family Favourites
1. Who were the first twins to both ride in the Epsom Derby, doing so in 1988?

2. They are the only father and son to do the double of 1000 runs and 100 wickets with New Zealand in Test matches. Name them.

3. This pair of brothers won Olympic titles and then held the world heavyweight title – but who are they?

4. Which brother and sister combination won the Wimbledon mixed doubles in 1980?

5. One of the 1999 athletics World Championship stars was Marion Jones, the 100 metres champion. Her husband also won gold – but who is he?

6. Name the father and son who both played in FA Cup Finals for Tottenham in the 1960s and 1980s, while another of the clan also played in the final for Tottenham?

7. A father and son combination enjoyed Aintree success in 1999 – one trained the National winner, the other rode the horse. Who are they?

8. And the scenario was repeated in 2000 – again, who trained the winner and who rode it?

9. A hard one now – which father and son have won British boxing's greatest belt, the heavyweight championship?

10. Who are the three sets of brothers who have played in the same FA Cup Final-winning sides against Liverpool?

11. Who were the last father and son to captain the England cricket team?

12. Since the war, only two fathers and sons have played for England in full internationals – who are they?

13. Who are the only father and son to be crowned world motor racing champion?

14. Scotland's two most capped rugby union players in the twentieth century were brothers – who are they?

15. Who are the brothers who in 2000 played for both Bradford Bulls and New Zealand?

16. This father was a legendary cricketer, while

his son also played county cricket and now plays rugby union in England – who are they?

17. These two brothers excelled for South Africa in the cricket arena, while a son of one of them plays today – their names, please?

18. Which pair of brothers played each other in a world snooker final – some year before John Parrott came on to the scene, mind you!

Quiz 7
Sporting Mastermind

1. Think About it
In a 147 snooker clearance, how many shots are made?

2. In Common
In 1988 what did Mike Gatting, John Emburey, Chris Cowdrey, Graham Gooch and Derek Pringle all do during the Test series against the West Indies?

3. FA Cup Finals
What have Kevin Reeves, Glenn Hoddle, Arnold Muhren and Eric Cantona all got in common?

4. Picture
Name the two famous sports stars that appear in this composite picture.

5. Name the Year
a) The FA Cup was won after a replay
b) Sally Gunnell set a world record in winning the world title

c) The Grand National was aborted and declared void

6. Who am I?
a) I was born in Plymouth in 1962 and won an Olympic medal in 1980
b) I was the Sports Writers' Sportswoman of the Year in 1978 and 1980 and returned to my sport after retirement in the 1990s
c) I was once the golden girl of British swimming

7. Think About it
Alfie Conn in 1977 became the first man in Scottish football history to have done what?

8. Who Said This?
Who in 1998 said, 'If I'd have had a gun at the time, I think I would have shot him'?

9. Frank answers
Name the three fighters who defeated Frank Bruno in world title fights?

10. Describe the Event
'With only eight minutes left, Bell and Lee combined and Alex Stepney was left distraught as the former King of Old Trafford casually . . .?

11. The Major Winners
Who are the four golfers who have won all four Majors?

12. Before You Go
Name the five England footballers whose surnames begin with the letter 'A' who have played in full internationals since 1980?

Sports Days

July

1. Who on 1 July 1977 became the last English player to win a Wimbledon singles championship?

2. After a record 125 England caps, which player ended his international career on 7 July 1990 in the third place play-off match against Italy in Bari?

3. Name the Englishman who scored 200 runs in just 219 balls against India on 9 July 1982.

4. In which sport did David Broome become Britain's first world champion on 10 July 1970?

5. One brother was born on 11 July 1953, the other on 13 July 1956 and they remain the only brothers to win Olympic titles and the world heavyweight title —but who are they?

6. Who on 7 July 1985 became the youngest ever winner of the Wimbledon men's singles aged only 17?

7. He won a world darts title in 1979, 1987 and 1993 and was born in Derbyshire on 21 July 1945 – can you name him?

8. Who on 21 July 1991 moved from Aston Villa to Bari for a British record fee of £5.5million?

9. Who in July 1988 won his Third Open Championship after a quite magnificent final round of 65?

10. Which English woman finally won the Wimbledon singles title at her thirteenth attempt on 4 July 1969?

11. By winning a play-off on 28 July 1987, she became the first British winner of the US Women's Open golf championships. Her name, please?

12. 30 July 1966 is a date imprinted on any sports fan's memory – but why?

13. Which partnership won a record fourth consecutive men's doubles title at Wimbledon on 6 July 1996?

14. Who on 3 July 1999 beat Tim Henman in the Wimbledon singles semi-finals for the second year running?

15. Who on 3 July 1997 followed his grandfather and father in playing Test cricket?

Local Heroes

North West Sport

1. Rugby League
Which club has supplied most players for Great Britain?

2. Athletics
Name the Liverpool sprinter who won a gold medal in the 4 x 400 metres relay in the European Championships and World Cup in 1998?

3. Football
In 1993 which manager was sacked as manager

of Manchester City just twelve days into the new season?

4. Rugby Union
Who played for Flyde and captained England 21 times between 1978 and 1982?

5. Football
Who managed Manchester City for just 33 days in 1996?

6. Rugby League
Who scored St Helens' only try in their Grand Final defeat of Bradford in 1999?

7. Football
Who in the 1990s became the only player to win both the European Cup Winners Cup and European Cup with the same English club?

8. Horse Racing
Who rode Freddie Starr's horse Miinehoma to Grand National victory in 1994?

9. Cricket
Who is the Lancashire wicket keeper who made two England Test appearances in 1998-99?

10. Football
Who was England's youngest player in the 1996 World Cup Final?

11. Golf
Which was the last Lancashire course to stage the Ryder Cup?

12. Rugby League
Which team did Martin Offiah join in the 2000 season?

13. Football
Who was the only player in the 1985 Everton v Man United FA Cup Final who never won an international cap?

14. Rugby Union
Who won 55 England caps from 1985 to 1993 and played his club rugby for Fylde and Preston Grasshoppers?

15. Cricket
Who was the great Lancashire fast bowler who was so often the opening partner of Yorkshire's Freddie Trueman for England?

Quiz 8
Sporting Mastermind

1. Who Said This?
Who in the late 1990s said: 'I have equalled Sir Don Bradman's record and that is enough for me'?

2. Who Am I?
a) I was born in 1942 in Scotland, and won my first jockey's title in 1972
b) I won the Derby on Troy, Henbit and Nashwan
c) I was once, like John Parrott, a captain of A *Question of Sport* with Bill Beaumont

3. In Which Year?
a) The Olympics were held in the USA
b) Damon Hill won a world title
c) Gareth Southgate's penalty miss meant that England missed out on a European Championship final?

4. Picture
This golfing great holds the record for major tournament wins. Who is he and how many?

5. What Happened Next?
'Liverpool, a goal down, had the chance to equalise when Brian Hill ruled that Goodyear had fouled Aldridge . . .'

6. How Many Players?
Do you find in –
a) A Gaelic football team
b) An American baseball team
c) An Australian Rules football team

7. In Common
Name the three players who've represented England at football since 1970 whose surnames begin with the letter 'O'.

8. Ian Botham
Name the three countries Ian Botham was with when capped by England?

9. The Name's the Same
a) A former England rugby captain, following Bill Beaumont
b) A fellow Evertonian friend of John Parrott who excels at the high jump?

10. Chelsea
In the same season in the 1990s, Chelsea had three Olympic gold medal winners in their squad – who were they?

11. Before You Go
Since 1970, eight players have contested a world snooker final with surnames ending in the letter 'S' – who are they?

Sports Days

August

1. Which athlete turned the tables on Steve Ovett by winning the Olympic 1500 metres title on 1 August 1980?

2. Who on 2 August 1987 beat IBF champion Tony Tucker to become the first undisputed world heavyweight champion since Leon Spinks in 1978?

3. 5 August 1978 saw Aberdeen play Tottenham in a friendly to inaugurate the first all-seater stadium in Britain. Can you name the ground?

4. On 7 August 1926 the first British Grand Prix was staged at which circuit?

5. Who on 9 August 1984 set a new decathlon world record in winning the Olympic title?

6. Despite being ninth reserve for the 1991 US PGA, this rookie won the title on 11 August by three strokes – who was he?

7. Who on 14 August 1948 went to the crease for the last time in Test cricket and was famously dismissed second ball by Eric Hollies?

8. The legendary 'Babe' Ruth died on 16 August 1948 aged 53. In which sport does he hold such status?

9. How did Charlton's Keith Peacock set a Football League first on 21 August 1965, something which has been repeated thousands of times since?

10. What 'first' was 'recorded' when Liverpool met Arsenal in the First Division on 22 August 1964?

11. What did Captain Matthew Webb take 21 hours and 45 minutes to do on 25 August 1875 which now takes less than eight hours to achieve?

12. Which British athlete won the European 100 metres gold medal on 19 August 1998?

13. Which country on 6 August 1997 reached 952 for 6 against India for the highest Test innings in history?

14. Which British athlete won the world decathlon silver medal on 25 August 1999?

15. For which county did Liam Botham take 5 for 67 on his first-class debut on 28 August 1996 against Middlesex?

Local Heroes

Welsh Sport

1. Football
Who was the last Welshman to captain the FA Cup winners at Wembley?

2. Golf
Who succeeded Nick Faldo as US Masters champion in 1991?

3. Cricket
Who captained Glamorgan to their County Championship win in 1997?

4. Rugby
Who captained Wales at both rugby union and rugby league and returned to union in 1995 from Warrington RLFC?

5. Football
Who was the first Welshman to win 90 international caps?

6. Boxing
Which Welsh boxer ended 1999 as WBO world super-middleweight champion?

7. Show Jumping
Which Welshman won the world title in 1970?

8. Athletics
Which Welshman won the 1998 Commonwealth Games 400 metres title?

9. Football
Who in January 1999 became the costliest Welshman when he joined Wimbledon for £7.5 million?

10. Rugby Union
This Welsh-born scrum half partnered Rob Andrew for England on 22 occasions – who is he?

11. Horse Racing
Where is the Welsh Grand National held?

12. Snooker
Name the two men who contested the first all-Welsh world final?

13. General
In which sport did Richie Burnett win a world title in 1995?

14. Football
Which Welsh boxer was the undefeated British featherweight champion from 1961 to 69 and also held a version of the world title?

15. Commonwealth Games
In which year were the Games held in Wales?

Quiz 9
Sporting Mastermind

1. Who Scored the Goal?
'With a minute left Emmerich hammered the free-kick against the English wall, Held blazed the rebound wildly across the English goal before . . .'

2. The Great Ali
Name the four British boxers who faced Muhammad Ali into the ring?

3. Picture
Name the two sports stars that appear in this composite picture.

4. In Common
Name the four former Everton players who managed Manchester City in the 1990s?

5. Who Comes Next?
In terms of the Olympic Games, who is next on this list in the twentieth century? Mary Rand, Ann Parker, Mary Peters, Tessa Sanderson?

6. Think About it
How did Maurice Revel inspire a pair of Olympic gold medal winners in 1984?

7. Who Am I?
a) I was born in 1964 and won the UK title and world title in 1991
b) I had previously won the European Open in 1989 and 1990
c) I have three passions: horse racing, Everton FC and working on this book!

8. Name the Year
1. Eric Cantona was sent off at Crystal Palace and banned for the rest of the season
2. South Africa won the rugby World Cup
3. Jonathan Edwards broke a world record at the World Championships

9. The Name's the Same
1. He played cricket for Surrey, Leciestershire and Nottingham as well as England
2. He lost in the 1983 Wimbledon singles final and comes from New Zealand

10. History Maker
How did Oliver Bierhoff's winning goal in the 1996 European Championship Final create history?

11. Before You Go
Name the eight British drivers who have won the Formula One world title?

Sports Days

September
1. In which event did Mary Peters pip Heide Rosendahl to win an athletics Olympic title on 3 September 1972?

2. Which famous cricket competition was first won on 7 September 1963 by Sussex?

3. Australian Lionel Van Praag became which sport's first world champion on 10 September 1936 at Wembley?

4. Who by winning the Italian Grand Prix on 10 September 1972 became the youngest ever world Formula One champion at just 25 years 273 days?

5. Born on 11 September 1950, he won the World 500cc Championship in 1976 and 1977 – can you name him?

6. Where did Tony Jacklin lead the Europeans to Ryder Cup success for the first time in 28 years on 15 September 1985?

7. The oldest of horse racing's Classics was run on 24 September 1776 at Doncaster. Which Classic was this?

8. Which legendary former manager died on 29 September 1981?

9. Which club did Liverpool defeat 9-0 at Anfield on 12 September 1989 when a record eight men scored in the game?

10. For the first time, a Classic was held in Scotland on 23 September 1989. Which course staged the St Leger that year?

11. On 24 September 1988, Ben Johnson won the Olympic 100 metres title but was disqualified following a drug offence – who was then proclaimed the gold medal winner?

12. Which cricket club clinched their first County Championship since 1971 on 2 September 1999?

13. On which horse did Pat Eddery record his 4,000th winner in Britain on 13 September 1997 when winning the St Leger?

14. Who on 12 September 1998 became the first American-born lady in 16 years to take the US Open tennis title?

15. Which Scotsman took gold in the 4,000 metres pursuit at the 1995 World Cycling Championships in Bogota on 27 September, to regain the title he won in 1993?

Local Heroes

Irish Sport

1. Football
Who was the goalkeeper who won 80 caps for the Republic of Ireland between 1981 and 1996?

2. Golf
Two Irishmen played in the 1999 Ryder Cup – name them.

3. Snooker
Name the three Irishmen who've won the world title at the Crucible?

4. Boxing
Who in 1995 ended Chris Eubank's 43–fight unbeaten record?

5. Football
Which current Scottish Premier League manager

captained Northern Ireland in the 1982 World Cup finals?

6. Horse Racing
Who rode Arkle to a hat-trick of Cheltenham Gold Cup victories?

7. Motor Racing
Which driver finished just two points behind world champion Mika Hakkinen in the 1999 Formula One Championship?

8. Rugby Union
Who scored a hat-trick of tries in the 2000 Six Nations Championship against France?

9. Football
Who was the last Irishman to captain the FA Cup winners at Wembley?

10. General
Which sport's principal championship is played in Croke Park, at 15-a-side, and see the winners lift the Sam Maguire Cup?

11. Golf
Which Irishman beat Tiger Woods to win the Golf Championship Matchplay in Carlsbad, California, in 2000?

12. Football
Who scored for Arsenal and Manchester United in FA Cup Finals in 1979 and 1983?

13. Athletics
Which Irish woman won the world 5,000 metres title in 1995?

14. Boxing
Which world champion's first name was Finbar,

although he used another Christian name in the ring?

15. Horse Racing
Where is the Irish Grand National run?

Quiz 10
Sporting Mastermind

1. Who Scored the Goal?
'With only 60 seconds of extra time to go, Gascoigne chipped a delicate free-kick to the right of the penalty spot and substitute . . .'

2. Who Said This?
'I assumed the box contained a Russian gift – I was in for a shock'

3. The Name's the Same
One rode Dr Devious to victory in the Derby, the other was a famous New Zealand cricketer – who are they?

4. Name the Year
1. Desert Orchid won the Cheltenham Gold Cup
2. Nick Faldo beat Scott Hoch in a play-off to win the Masters
3. Arsenal won at Anfield to take the League Championship in the last minute of the final game of the season

5. Who am I?
1. I was born in Bath in 1965 and made my England debut in Romania in 1989
2. I helped my club to a Pilkington Cup win in 1987, the first of many victories for me

3. I partnered Will Carling in the centre on many occasions for England

6. Picture
Currently Manchester United's longest serving player, but at which Football League club did his career begin in 1983?

7. Think About it
Who in 1990 became the first on-loan player to win an FA Cup winners' medal?

8. Left-Handers
Who are the four left-handed Wimbledon men's singles champions since 1960?

9. Before You Go
Since 1970 seven Wimbledon singles champions – male and female – have had a surname which ends in a vowel. Can you name them?

Sports Days

October

1. By what name is Muhammad Ali's fight with Joe Frazier, on 1 October 1985 which Ali won at the end of the 14th round, affectionately known?

2. He was born on 5 October 1946 in South Africa and after captaining England he joined Kerry Parker's rebel cricketers in the 1970s – who is he?

3. Which former manager of Preston was born on 11 October 1937 and went on to win World Cup and European Cup winners' medals?

4. Which British athlete won the Olympic 400 metres hurdles title on 15 October 1968?

5. Born Edson Arantes de Nascimento on 23 October 1940, he is better known by what name?

6. Who was jailed on 23 October 1987 for tax offences but was released after serving a third of his three-year sentence?

7. On 24 October 1987 this 37-year-old fighter's attempt to regain the British heavyweight title was thwarted in the eighth round by defending champion Frank Bruno. Name him.

8. 'Steady Eddie' was born 31 October 1929 and he twice made a World Snooker Final. Who is he?

9. Which player on 1 October 1977 played his last senior game for New York Cosmos against his former club Santos of Brazil?

10. On 9 October 1988 Wally Lewis led which country to victory in the Rugby League World Cup Final against New Zealand?

11. Who on 13 October 1984 became the first darts thrower to record a 501 nine-dart finish to win £102,000 in the World Matchplay Championship?

12. Sagamix gave which jockey his third successive winner of the Prix de l'Arc de Triomphe on 10 October 1977?

13. In which sport did Briton Kate Howey win a world title on 10 October 1997?

14. Which South African kicked a record five drop goals in the 1999 Rugby World Cup quarter-final against England on 24 October 1999?

15. And which country shocked the world by beating New Zealand in the Rugby World Cup on 31 October 1999?

Local Heroes

Scottish Sport

1. Football
Which club in 1999-2000 was defeated in both the Scottish FA Cup final and League Cup final?

2. Cricket
For which county does Test player Gavin Hamilton play?

3. Motor Racing
Who was the last Scotsman to win the Monaco Grand Prix to David Coulthard in 2000?

4. Golf
Who was the only Briton to play in all the Ryder Cup competitions in the 1990s?

5. Football
Since the formation of the Scottish Premier Division in 1975-76, which two clubs, besides Rangers and Celtic, have won the title?

6. Rugby Union
Name the two Scotsmen who captained the British Lions in 1989 and 1993 respectively?

7. Boxing
Two Scotsmen held versions of the world

lightweight title in the 1970s – name them.

8. Football
Who in 1986 replaced Kenny Dalglish in Scotland's World Cup squad and also played in the European Cup Final that year?

9. Snooker
Only two Scotsmen won the world title at the Crucible between 1977 and 2000 – Stephen Hendry and who else?

10. Motor Racing
Who was the first Scotsman to be crowned world champion?

11. Football
Which Scottish striker scored goals in the World Cup Finals in 1974, 1978 and 1982?

12. Athletics
Who is the only Scotsman to have won the Olympic 100 metres title?

13. General
In which sport did Richard Corsie win three indoor world titles between 1989 and 1993?

14. Horse Racing
Sharing its name with a Scottish football club, this horse won two English Classics for Willie Carson in 1977 – name it.

15. Golf
Two Scotsmen made their debuts in the 1999 Ryder Cup – name them.

Quiz 11
Sporting Mastermind

1. Describe the Event
'With 55 yards to go and the race at his mercy, royalty witnessed the greatest disaster in over 100 years of Aintree history when . . .'

2. Who Am I?
1. I was born in 1966 and made my professional debut in 1985
2. I won the WBO middleweight title in 1990 and the WBO super-middleweight crown in 1991
3. In 1995 Steve Collins ended my unbeaten record and took the world super-middleweight crown?

3. Name the Year
1. Bjorn Borg won his last Wimbledon singles title
2. Nottingham Forest played in their third successive League Cup Final
3. Coe, Ovett, Wells and Thompson won Olympic gold?

4. In Common
Only four footballers since the war with surnames beginning with the letter 'V' have won full England caps – who are they?

5. Who Said This?
Who, after winning a US Women's golf tournament, remarked, after receiving no congratulations from the Minister of Sport Tony Banks: The only Banks I've heard from is the NatWest'?

6. Think About it
What particular feat did Alec Stewart achieve in the Third Test against the West Indies in 2000, which only Colin Cowdrey (1968), Javed Miandad (1989) and Gordon Greenidge (1990) had previously achieved?

7. Cup Heroes
Name the two English football clubs which have contained three World Cup winners in their line-up.

8. Before You Go
Since Peter Thomson in 1965, ten non-American golfers have won the Open Championship – who are they?

Sports Days

November

1. Which Rugby union player scored an English record 23 points against Argentina on 3 November 1990 to beat Douglas Lambert's 79-year-old record by one?

2. For which club did Adcock, Stewart and White all score a hat-trick in a 10-1 win on 7 November 1987?

3. Which LA Lakers basketball star shocked the American nation with the announcement that he was HIV-positive on 7 November 1991?

4. Which player on 11 November 1986 lost his first match in over five years against Ross Norman in the final of the World Open squash championship?

5. The first gymnast to score a maximum 10 points in international competition, this star of the 1976 Montreal Olympics was born on 12 November 1961 – who is she?

6. On 13 November 1992 Evander Holyfield lost his world heavyweight title to which boxer in Las Vegas?

7. Which player bowed out of international soccer on 14 November 1973 against Italy at Wembley after 108 England games?

8. Who 15 November 1989 became the first £1 million goalkeeper when he left Bristol Rovers?

9. On 8 November 1987 Australia beat England to win cricket's World cup – but who captained the Aussies?

10. Which country on 25 November 1953 handed England their first defeat by a continental side at Wembley?

11. Can you name the former British world motor racing champion who was killed in an aircrash on 29 November 1975?

12. On 6 November 1999 who captained Australia to victory in the Rugby World Cup against France?

13. Which coach in November 1999 was sacked at Real Madrid for the second time?

14. Which boxer beat Simona Lukic in the first officially sanctioned women's professional bout in the UK on 25 November 1998?

15. Who on 10 November 1995 took the World Open squash title for a record seventh time, beating Briton Del Harris in the final?

Local Heroes

Yorkshire Sport

1. Snooker
Who did Steve Davis meet in successive World Championship Finals in the 1980s?

2. Football
Who was the first Leeds United player to score in an FA Cup Final?

3. Cricket
He played 46 Tests for England and his brother won 16 caps at fly half for the England rugby union side – who are they?

4. Boxing
Which Yorkshireman fought for the world heavyweight title in 1976 against Muhammad Ali?

5. General
At which sport did Briton Anita Lonsbrough win an Olympic gold medal in 1960?

6. Football
Which club was managed by Emlyn Hughes when they were relegated in 1983?

7. Horse Racing
Stravinsky won the 1999 Nunthorpe Stakes – but where is the race run?

8. Rugby League
Which club won their first major title, the Challenge Cup, in 1998?

9. Football
Who were the last club to score in the FA Cup Final and still lose?

10. Rugby Union
Who in 1994 became the first Englishman to accomplish every possible method of scoring in the same game – try, drop goal, penalty and conversion?

11. Boxing
Who was the Sheffield-born boxer who defeated Steven Robinson to take the WBO world featherweight title in 1995?

12. Football
Name the three Leeds United players of the Revie era who went on to manage the club in the 1980s.

13. Lawn Tennis
Which player appeared in three Wimbledon men's singles semi-finals between 1967 and 1973?

14. Cricket
Who played for England in 1949 and made his last Test appearance 27 years later?

15. Football
Who was the only player to score 30 Premiership goals in 1999-2000?

Quiz 12
Sporting Mastermind

1. In Common
What particular fact links cricket counties Sussex, Northants, Durham and Somerset?

2. Controlling body
Which sport's governing body is the WPBSA?

3. Boxing Macs
In the 1980s four British boxers beginning with a Mc or Mac held a world title – who are they?

4. In What Year?
a) Europe held on to the Ryder Cup
b) Nick Faldo won his first Open at Muirfield
c) Coventry won the FA Cup for the first time

5. Who Said This?
Which football chairman said in 1999: 'I believe in Methusaleh, alien beings, flying saucers and the Hand of God. But most of all I believe in on-loan goalkeepers from Swindon scoring in the 95th minute'?

6. Think About it
Children (and adults) enjoy colouring in letters, but which English club's name can you not colour in?

7. Who Scored the Goal?
'Four minutes later he repeated the feat, but this time with a goal of sheer class as he skipped past Reid, Fenwick and Butcher before flicking the ball past Shilton . . .'

8. The Name's the Same
A former Ipswich and England forward and a current Ipswich forward share the same name – what is it?

9. Who Am I?
1. I was born in Manchester in 1968 and played for Cambridge University from 1987 to 1989
2. I became England captain in 1993
3. I am still a regular opening batsman with Lancashire

10. Before You Go
By the end of the West Indies series in 2000 Michael Atherton had had 13 opening partners in Test matches – who are they?

Sports Days

December
1. One of golf's great characters was born on 1 December 1939. He won the Championship in 1971 and 1972 – who was he?

2. Which country on 1 December 1991 won the Davis Cup in tennis for the first time since 1932?

3. Ireland's most capped rugby union international was born on 3 December 1943. He won 69 caps between 1964 and 1979 – but who is he?

4. How did the First Division match between Newcastle and Portsmouth make history on 5 December 1931?

5. The one-time golden girl of British athletics died of cancer on 26 December 1970 aged only 22 – who was she?

6. Which National Hunt trainer saddled a record 12 winners in a single day on 27 December 1982?

7. Who was the German who on 8 December 1991 became the first official World Footballer of the Year?

8. Between 9 December and 14 December 1961, Australia and West Indies played out cricket's first tied Test match. Who were the two captains?

9. Which Englishman on 23 December 1981 passed Garry Sobers' world record Test run aggregate?

10. Where did the Republic of Ireland lose 2-0 to Holland on 13 December 1995 in a play-off for Euro 96?

11. Which British woman claimed her first major senior title by winning the European Cross-Country Championships in Italy on 12 December 1998?

12. Which Australian rugby international made his 101st and final appearance in the 28-19 victory over Wales at the Arms Park on 1 December 1996?

13. Who on 1 December 1999 was named as

the new Ryder Cup captain for the European team?

14. Which National Hunt jockey on 11 December 1999 became the fastest jockey to record 1,000 winners after victory on Majdou?

15. Who on 29 December 1994 took a hat-trick for Australia against England?

Local Heroes

General Sport

1. Horse Racing
Which is the only horse to have won the Aintree, Scottish and Welsh Grand Nationals?

2. Football
In 1998 who became the first player to appear in games for both Merseyside and both Manchester clubs?

3. Motor Cycling
It is nearly 25 years since a Briton won the coveted world 500cc title. Who achieved this feat in 1977?

4. Golf
What is unique, among all the Open Championship winners, about Bob Charles, the winner in 1963?

5. Football
Only one player scored a hat-trick against England in Peter Shilton's 125 games in goal for his country. Who did this in the 1988 European Championships?

6. Snooker
Only two overseas players won the world title at the Crucible from 1977 to 1999 inclusive – one was Ken Doherty, who was the other?

7. Cricket
Who captained England in the 1999 World Cup?

8. Motor Racing
Hockenheim staged the 1999 German Grand Prix – but which German circuit staged the European Grand Prix?

9. Rugby Union
Who in 1995 had a 'whale' of a time against England by scoring four tries in a World Cup match?

10. Football
Which player in 1980 left Arsenal and went on to play for four different Italian clubs?

And Finally

1. Since 1985, four men have managed the FA Cup winners having previously played for the same club in an FA Cup winning side – who are they?

2. Who are the three players who've been named the European Footballer of the Year on three occasions?

3. Who are the three players with a 'V' in their surname who scored in an FA Cup Final in the 1980s?

4. Who managed a Championship-winning side in England while his brother did likewise in Scottish football?

5. Which member of England's 1966 World Cup winning side played in over 100 League games for four different English clubs?

6. Besides Derby and Nottingham Forest, which other three clubs did Brian Clough manage?

7. By the end of the 1999-2000 season, six players had scored 100 Premier League goals – name them.

8. Which international goalkeeper played in League Cup Finals in England with three different clubs in three different decades – 1970s, 1980s and 1990s?

9. Which three sides have beaten Manchester United in a League Cup Final?

10. Four players between 1983 and 2000 scored five goals in a match in the top flight in England – but who are they?

11. Former England manager Graham Taylor managed four League sides – which ones?

12. Five men have managed Chelsea in the Premiership – who are they?

13. Which four clubs have returned to the League after dropping into the Conference since re-election was abolished?

14. Sir Alex Ferguson managed three clubs prior to Manchester United – name them.

15. In the 1966 World Cup, England played six countries. West Germany were one, but who were the other five?

Sporting Mastermind Answers

Quiz 1

1. Roberto di Matteo (1997 FA Cup Final)
2. New Zealand
3. In the abortive 1993 Grand National, White 'won' on Esha Ness' and Captain Brown was the starter
4. George Graham
5. 1996
6. Brian Clough, Middlesbrough
7. David O'Leary
8. Dave Watson
9. Warren Barton, Alan Shearer, Barry Venison, David Batty, Peter Beardsley, Chris Waddle, Les Ferdinand, Steve Howey, Robert Lee and Kieron Dyer

Quiz 2

1. Paul Gascoigne's injury in the 1991 FA Cup Final
2. Stefan Edberg
3. Man United – League and Cup double winners
4. Darts
5. 1998
6. Winning the Featherweight gold medal at the Commonwealth Games
7. John Barnes
8. Tommy Smith
9. Sunderland – Michael Gray, Kevin Phillips, Nick Pickering, Tony Towers, Dave Watson Middlesbrough – David Armstrong, Nick Barmby, Paul Gascoigne, Paul Ince, Paul Merson, Gary Pallister

Quiz 3

1. Iuean Evans
2. Silverstone, Aintree and Brands Hatch
3. Roger Bannister's four-minute mile
4. David Coleman
5. Youngest Welsh international
6. He won Winter and Summer gold medals
7. 1987
8. Brian Moore
9. Croquet
10. Hon. Lionel Tennyson (1889–1951)
11. Paul Gascoigne, Mark Hateley, Paul Ince, Gary Lineker, Steve McManaman, David Platt, Trevor Steven, Chris Waddle, Des Walker, Glenn Hoddle

Quiz 4

1. 1990
2. Granfranco Zola

(1998 European Cup
Winners Cup Final)
3. They all reached the
final while in Division
Two
4. He never won a world
title fight
5. Joe Royle (the rest
were all goalkeepers)
6. Sharron Davies/Tiger
Woods
7. John Salako, Tony
Cascarino, Scott
Minto, Roberto di
Matteo, Juninho,
Nolberton Solano
8. Steve Davis
9. Swimming (1.5km),
cycling (4km), running
(10km)
10. Robert Jones
11. Peter Barnes, Colin
Bell, Mick Channon,
Joe Corrigan, Keith
Curle, Mike Doyle,
Trevor Francis,
Rodney Marsh, Kevin
Reeves, Joe Royle,
Mike Summerbee,
Denis Tueart, Dave
Watson, David White,
Francis Lee

Quiz 5

1. Paul Lawrie talking
about Jean Van de
Velde
2. 1992 Ian Rush played
for Liverpool, David
Rush for Sunderland
3. John Regis in the
1991 World
Championship 4 x 400
Relay team which won
the Gold medal for
Great Britain

4. All use a net – but no
ball
5. 1990 World Cup:
Germany goal v
England
6. Lennox Lewis, Herbie
Hide, Frank Bruno,
Henry Akinwande
7. Kevin Keegan, Mick
Mills, Alan Ball, Mick
Channon, Dave
Watson
8. 1985
9. Ayrton Senna, San
Marino, Italy
10. Colin Montgomerie
11. Gordon Cowans, Earl
Barrett, Steve Hodge,
Tony Morley, Nigel
Spink, Kevin
Richardson, Peter
Withe, Tony Daley,
Ugo Ehiogu, Dion
Dublin, Lee Hendrie,
David Platt, Gareth
Southgate, Gareth
Barry, Stan Collymore,
Paul Merson

Quiz 6

1. Geoff Boycott
2. Archie Gemmill (v
Holland, 1978)
3. Nobby Stiles, Martin
Peters, George Cohen
4. Steve Cram
5. 1982
6. Their fathers all played
for England
7. France
8. Alan Mullery (for
Tottenham and
Fulham)
9. a) Detroit b) New York
c) Edmonton
10. Peter Thompson, Kel

Nagle, Ian Baker-
Finch, Greg Norman
11. Gary Mabbutt, Nicky
Butt, Luther Blissett,
Terry McDermott,
David Platt, Earl
Barrett

Quiz 7

1. 36
2. All captained England
3. All scored penalties
4. Mike Tyson/Frankie
Dettori
5. 1993
6. Sharron Davies
7. Win the Scottish Cup
with both Rangers and
Celtic
8. John Gregory over
Dwight Yorke's
transfer to
Manchester United
9. Tim Witherspoon,
Mike Tyson, Lennox
Lewis
10. Denis Law's goal for
Man City sent Man
Utd into Division Two
11. Ben Hogan, Gene
Sarazen, Gary Player,
Jack Nicklaus
12. Darren Anderton,
David Armstrong,
Tony Adams, Clive
Allen, Viv Anderson

Quiz 8

1. Mark Taylor
2. Willie Carson
3. 1996
4. Jack Nicklaus,
Eighteen
5. John Aldridge missed

a 1988 FA Cup Final
penalty
6. a) 15 b) 9 c) 18
7. Michael Owen, Peter
Osgood, Russell
Osman
8. Somerset,
Worcestershire and
Durham
9. Steve Smith
10. Celestine Babayaro,
Dmitri Kharine, Albert
Ferrer
11. Alex Higgins, Terry
Griffiths, Steve Davis,
John Higgins, Mark
Williams, Graham
Miles, Perrie Mans,
Matthew Stevens

Quiz 9

1. German equaliser (2-
2) in 1966 World Cup
Final
2. Henry Cooper, Brian
London, Joe Bugner,
Richard Dunn
3. Martina Navratilova/
Jonah Lomu
4. Alan Ball, Howard
Kendall, Peter Reid,
Joe Royle
5. Sally Gunnell (British
woman gold medallist
in athletics)
6. His Bolero music was
used by Torvill and
Dean
7. John Parrott
8. 1995
9. Chris Lewis
10. It was the first Golden
Goal to decide a
championship
11. Mike Hawthorn,
Graham Hill, Jim

Clark, John Surtees,
Jackie Stewart, James
Hunt, Nigel Mansell,
Damon Hill

Quiz 10

1. David Platt (England v
Belgium, 1990 World
Cup)
2. Alex Ferguson
3. John Reid
4. 1989
5. Jeremy Guscott
6. Denis Irwin, Leeds
United
7. Les Sealey
(Manchester United)
8. Neale Fraser, Rod
Laver, John McEnroe,
Jimmy Connors
9. Virginia Wade,
Martina Navratilova,
Jana Novotna, Andre
Agassi, John
McEnroe, Arthur
Ashe, John
Newcombe

Section 11

1. Devon Loch fell in the
1956 Grand National
2. Chris Eubank
3. 1980
4. Terry Venables, Barry
Venison, Colin Vilijoen
and Denis Viollet
5. Laura Davies
6. They are the four
players who have
scored a century in
their 100th Test
match
7. West Ham United
(1966-67) and

Chelsea (1999-2000)
8. Paul Lawrie, Nick
Price, Greg Norman,
Nick Faldo, Ian Baker-
Finch, Seve
Ballesteros, Sandy
Lyle, Gary Player, Tony
Jacklin, Roberto de
Vicenzo

Quiz 12

1. They have not won the
County Championship
2. Billiards and snooker
3. Glenn McCrory, Duke
McKenzie, Dave
McAuley and Barry
McGuigan
4. 1987
5. Michael Knighton,
Carlisle United
chairman, after his
club had narrowly
avoided relegation
from the football
league
6. Hull City
7. Diego Maradona
(1986 World Cup v
England)
8. David Johnson
9. Michael Atherton
10. Graham Gooch, Mark
Lathwell, Wayne
Larkins, Alec Stewart,
Robin Smith, Nick
Knight, Mark Butcher,
Jason Gallian, Steve
James, Darren
Maddy, John Crawley,
Mark Ramprakash,
Marcus Trescothick

Sports Days Answers

Quiz 1

January
1. Sir Stanley Matthews
2. Eric Bristow
3. Floyd Patterson
4. Kapil Dev
5. Harlem Globetrotters
6. Stephen Hendry
7. Muhammad Ali
8. Steve Backley
9. Jock Stein
10. Sutton United
11. Stefan Edberg
12. Steven Davis
13. Jack Nicklaus
14. Bob Paisley
15. David Duval

Quiz 2

February
1. Trevor Francis
2. Shergar
3. Sandy Lyle
4. Kevin Keegan
5. Peter Scudamore
6. Bobby Robson
7. Kenny Dalglish
8. Cassius Clay/Muhammad Ali
9. The Grand National
10. Allan Border
11. Barry McGuigan
12. Eric Cantona
13. Nicolas Anelka
14. Manchester United
15. Ashia Hansen

Quiz 3

March
1. Garry Sobers
2. Dixie Dean
3. Kenny Dalglish
4. Lennox Lewis
5. Sergei Bubka
6. Michael Dickinson
7. Alex Higgins and Pat Eddery
8. Ayrton Senna
9. Jesse Owens
10. Shaun Edwards
11. Joe Frazier
12. John Carleton
13. Torvill and Dean
14. Courtney Walsh
15. Wilson Kipketer

Quiz 4

April
1. Red Rum
2. John Virgo
3. 1981
4. Olympic Games
5. Seve Ballesteros
6. Tottenham Hotspur
7. Steve Davis
8. Rocky Marciano
9. Andy Gregory
10. Chelsea
11. Nigel Mansell
12. Jimmy White
13. Peter Nicol
14. Wayne Gretzky
15. Tiger Woods

Quiz 5

May

1. Betting shops were made legal
2. He won an FA Cup winners' medal
3. The Derby
4. Roger Bannister
5. John Parrott
6. Olga Korbut
7. Real Madrid
8. Henry Cooper
9. Jesse Owens
10. The TT race
11. They reached the summit of Everest
12. Viv Richards
13. Leeds Utd
14. Graeme Hick
15. Table Tennis

Quiz 6

June

1. Lester Piggott
2. The Ryder Cup
3. Ed Moses
4. He was the first England player ever to be sent off
5. Monica Seles
6. Seb Coe
7. Pat Jennings
8. Giacomo Agostini
9. Ian Botham
10. Tony Jacklin
11. Australia
12. Real Madrid
13. Gustavo Kuerton
14. Andre Agassi
15. Dickie Bird

Quiz 7

July

1. Virginia Wade
2. Peter Shilton
3. Ian Botham
4. Show jumping
5. Michael and Leon Spinks
6. Boris Becker
7. John Lowe
8. David Platt
9. Seve Ballesteros
10. Ann Jones
11. Laura Davies
12. England won the World Cup
13. Todd Woodbridge and Mark Woodforde
14. Pete Sampras
15. Dean Headley

Quiz 8

August

1. Seb Coe
2. Mike Tyson
3. Pittodrie
4. Brooklands
5. Daley Thompson
6. John Daly
7. Don Bradman
8. Baseball
9. He came on as a substitute
10. Match of the Day
11. Swim the English Channel
12. Darren Campbell
13. Sri Lanka
14. Dean macey
15. Hampshire

Quiz 9

September
1. Pentathlon
2. Gillette Cup
3. Speedway
4. Emerson Fittipaldi
5. Barry Sheene
6. The Belfry
7. The St Leger
8. Bill Shankly
9. Crystal Palace
10. Ayr
11. Carl Lewis
12. Surrey
13. Silver Patriarch
14. Lindsay Davenport
15. Graeme Obree

Quiz 10

October
1. The 'Thriller in Manila'
2. Tony Greig
3. Bobby Charlton
4. David Hemery
5. Pele
6. Lester Piggott
7. Joe Bugner
8. Eddie Charlton
9. Pele
10. Australia
11. John Lowe
12. Olivier Peslier
13. Judo
14. Jannie de Beer
15. France

Quiz 11

November
1. Simon Hodgkinson
2. Manchester City
3. Magic Johnson
4. Jahangir Khan
5. Nadia Comaneci
6. Riddick Bowe
7. Bobby Moore
8. Nigel Martyn
9. Allan Border
10. Hungary
11. Graham Hill
12. John Eales
13. John Toshack
14. Jane Couch
15. Jansher Khan

Quiz 12

December
1. Lee Trevino
2. France
3. Mike Gibson
4. No corners were recorded
5. Lillian Board
6. Michael Dickinson
7. Lothar Matthaus
8. Frank Worrell (WI) and Richie Benaud (Aus)
9. Geoff Boycott
10. Anfield
11. Paula Radcliffe
12. David Campese
13. Sam Torrance
14. Tony McCoy
15. Shane Warne

Local Heroes Answers

Quiz 1

Firsts

1. American football's Super Bowl
2. Daley Thompson
3. Wilt Chamberlain
4. Heavyweight boxing
5. Sunil Gavaskar
6. Real Madrid
7. Lester Piggott
8. John Curry
9. Frans Thijssen
10. Mike Hawthorn
11. St Helens
12. Bath
13. John Spencer
14. Richard Krajicek
15. Stanley Matthews

Quiz 2

Midlands Sport

1. Sutton United
2. Tessa Sanderson
3. Dominic Cork
4. Trevor Francis
5. Brian Moore
6. WBA (1968) and Coventry (1987)
7. Rugby union (Dusty Hare)
8. Richie Woodhall
9. Bayern Munich
10. Fred Davis
11. Steve Bull
12. Tony Barton
13. Martin Johnson
14. Pat Cowdell
15. Dermot Reeve

Quiz 3

London Sport

1. Ruud Gullit (AC Milan) and Petrescu (Steava Bucharest)
2. Lawrence Dallaglio
3. Leeds
4. Adam and Ben Hollioake
5. Jimmy Greaves
6. London Welsh
7. Frank Bruno
8. Denis Compton
9. Basketball
10. Alf Ramsey, Terry Venables and Glenn Hoddle
11. Seb Coe
12. Vinnie Jones
13. Darts
14. Henry Akinwande
15. Shaun Edwards and Martin Offiah

Quiz 4

North East Sport

1. Dave Watson
2. Glen McCrory
3. Brian Lara (501)
4. Brendan Foster
5. Jack Charlton
6. Gosforth
7. Ice Hockey
8. Holland
9. Fabrizio Ravanelli (Middlesbrough)
10. Shaun McCrae
11. Sue Rolph
12. Alan Shearer
13. Billy Hardy

14. Liam Botham
15. Steve Cram

Quiz 5

Merseyside Sport
1. Ian Rush
2. John Conteh
3. Grand National
4. Birkdale
5. Mark Hughes
6. John Parrott
7. Waterloo
8. John Toshack
9. Chris Boardman
10. St Helens

Quiz 6

Family Favourites
1. Richard and Michael Hills
2. Lance and Chris Cairns
3. Michael and Leon Spinks
4. Tracy and John Austin
5. CJ Hunter
6. Les and Clive Allen. Paul Allen also played for Spurs
7. Tommy and Paul Carberry
8. Ted and Ruby Walsh
9. Jack and Brian London
10. Leslie and Denis Compton (Arsenal 1950) Brian and Jimmy Greenhoff (Man Utd 1977) Gary and Phil Neville (Man Utd 1996)
11. Colin and Chris Cowdrey
12. Brian and Nigel Clough

Frank Jnr and Frank Snr Lampard
13. Graham and Damon Hill
14. Gavin and Scott Hastings
15. Robbie and Henry Paul
16. Liam and Ian Botham
17. Graeme and Peter Pollock. Peter's son is Shaun
18. Joe and Fred Davis

Quiz 7

North West Sport
1. Wigan
2. Alyn Condon
3. Peter Reid
4. Bill Beaumont
5. Steve Coppell
6. Kevin Iro
7. Denis Irwin
8. Richard Dunwoody
9. Warren Hegg
10. Alan Ball
11. Royal Lytham
12. Salford
13. Derek Mountfield (Everton)
14. Wade Dooley
15. Brian Statham

Quiz 8

Welsh Sport
1. Kevin Ratcliffe (Everton 1984)
2. Ian Woosman
3. Matthew Maynard
4. Jonathan Davies
5. Neville Southall
6. Joe Calzaghe
7. David Broome
8. Iwan Thomas
9. John Hartson

10. Dewi Morris
11. Chepstow
12. Mark Williams and Matthew Stevens
13. Darts
14. Howard Winstone
15. 1958

Quiz 9

Irish Sport

1. Pat Bonner
2. Darren Clarke and Padraig Harrington
3. Alex Higgins, Dennis Taylor and Ken Doherty
4. Steve Collins
5. Martin O'Neill
6. Pat Eddery
7. Eddie Irvine
8. Brian O'Driscoll
9. Roy Keane
10. Gaelic football
11. Darren Clarke
12. Frank Stapleton
13. Sonia O'Sullivan
14. Barry McGuigan
15. Fairyhouse

Quiz 10

Scottish Sport

1. Aberdeen
2. Yorkshire
3. Jackie Stewart
4. Colin Montgomerie
5. Aberdeen and Dundee Utd
6. Finlay Calder and Gavin Hastings
7. Jim Watt and Ken Buchanan
8. Steve Archibald
9. John Higgins
10. Jim Clark

11. Joe Jordan
12. Allan Wells
13. Bowls
14. Dunfermline
15. Paul Lawrie and Andrew Coltart

Quiz 11

Yorkshire Sport

1. Joe Johnson
2. Billy Bremner (1965)
3. Chris and Alan Old
4. Richard Dunn
5. Swimming
6. Rotherham United
7. York
8. Sheffield Eagles
9. Sheffield Wednesday (1993)
10. Rob Andrew
11. Prince Naseem Hamed
12. Allan Clarke, Billy Bremner and Eddie Gray
13. Roger Taylor
14. Brian Close
15. Kevin Phillips

Quiz 12

General Sport

1. Earth Summit
2. Peter Beardsley
3. Barry Sheene
4. He was left-handed
5. Marco Van Basten (Holland)
6. Cliff Thorburn (Canada)
7. Alec Stewart
8. The Nurburgring
9. Jonah Lomu
10. Liam Brady

And Finally Answers

1. Terry Venables (Tottenham), Kenny Dalglish (Liverpool), Gianluca Vialli (Chelsea), George Graham (Arsenal)
2. Michael Platini, Johan Cruyff and Marco Van Basten
3. Kevin Reeves (Man City 1981), Ricky Villa (Tottenham 1981) and Gary Stevens (Brighton 1983)
4. Bill Shankly (Liverpool) Bob Shankly (Dundee)
5. Alan Ball (Blackpool, Everton, Arsenal, Southampton)
6. Hartlepool, Brighton and Leeds Utd
7. Alan Shearer, Andy Cole, Les Ferdinand, Ian Wright, Robbie Fowler and Matthew Le Tissier
8. Chris Wood (Nottingham Forest, Norwich City, Sheffield Wednesday)
9. Liverpool (1983), Sheffield Wednesday (1991) and Aston Villa (1994)
10. Ian Rush, Tony Woodcock, Andy Cole and Alan Shearer
11. Lincoln, Aston Villa, Wolves and Watford
12. Ian Porterfield, David Webb, Glenn Hoddle, Ruud Gullit, Gianluca Vialli
13. Lincoln, Darlington, Halifax and Colchester
14. East Stirlingshire, St Mirren and Aberdeen
15. Uruguay, Mexico, France, Argentina and Portugal

Did You Know . . .?

Now you've tested yourself in the Quiz Sections, we've put together some sporting trivia which will add to your knowledge of the world of sport.

They're unusual, thought-provoking and, of course, informative. Why not use them to set your own questions?

Athletics

- In 1996 Merlene Ottey competed in her fifth Olympic 200 metres final. She won three bronze medals and a silver, while in 1988 she finished in fourth place.

- In the 1999 World Championships, Marion Jones won the women's 100 metres while her husband CJ Hunter won the men's shot putt. CJ's Christian name is Cottrell.

- Jurgen Schult in 1999 became the only man to compete in all seven World Championships, doing so in the discus.

- Michael Johnson in 1999 became the first man to hold the 200 metres and 400 metres World Record since the 'Black Power' runner Tommie Smith in the 1960s.

- Nova Peris-Kneebone won the Commonwealth 200 metres title in 1998. In 1996 she was in Australia's Olympic hockey gold medal-winning side.

- Czech tennis star Hana Mandlikova's father Vilem Mandlik was fourth in the 1958 European 200 metres.

- Author and politician Jeffry Archer represented Great Britain against Sweden in 1966 in the sprints. He was also an Oxford Blue at athletics.

- Singer Johnny Mathis, who has topped the charts in the UK, was ranked No 85 in the world high jump in 1955 with a height of 1.97m/6'.

- Top commentator David Coleman won the 1949 Manchester Mile and won a third-place team medal at the 1952 English National Cross-Country Championships.

- Starting blocks were perfected in 1927 and introduced into major championships in 1929 at the NCAA Championships in Chicago.

- Vyncheslav Skomorokhov won the 400 metres hurdles at the 1969 European Championships. He was a deaf mute.

- When Abebe Bikila won the 1960 Olympic marathon, he did so in bare feet. In 1964 he repeated the gold medal-winning performance, but this time wore shoes.

- The first woman to be disqualified for failing a sex test was Olympic and European sprint medallist Ewa Klobukowska in 1967 at the Europa Cup final.

- In the time of amateur athletics, Olympic 110 metres hurdles gold medallist Lee Calhoun was suspended for a year after he had been married on the Bride and Groom television show in August 1957. His bride won $2,500 worth of gifts and a $6,000 swimming pool.

Calhoun returned to competition and won the Olympic title again in 1960.

- Marshall Brooks in 1876 was the first man to high jump 6ft – Charles Dumas in 1956 registered the first 7ft jump while Cuban Javier Satomayor in 1993 broke the 8ft barrier.

- By 1 January 2000, the only men's world records in an Olympic event dating back to the 1980s belonged to Jurgen Schult (discus) and Yury Sedykh (hammer).

- By 1 January 2000 Britain had two world record holders – Colin Jackson and Jonathan Edwards – in Olympic events. The 4 x 800 metres record of 1982 was still held by Peter Elliott, Gary Cook, Steve Cram and Seb Coe.

Boxing

- In the 1970s American journalist Elliott Harvith reported on the meteoric rise of Jewish heavyweight prospect Sol Nazleman – of whom he was the manager – who had recorded 30 consecutive knockout victories in obscure venues in Wichita and Arkansas. The young fighter appeared in the fight ratings and attracted interest from nationwide TV networks. There was a problem: Nazleman did not exist and had been invented by the devious hack to test the gullibility of the boxing authorities. To avoid detection, Harvith arranged for his protégé to be 'killed' in a car crash and then was paid by various newspapers to write his obituary!

- The April heavyweight title clash between **Lennox Lewis** and **Michael Grant** was the heaviest title fight in history, with the two having a combined weight of 497lb (over 35 stone). The previous record of 489lb had been set in 1933 when **Primo Carnera** (Italy) met **Paulino Uzcudan** (Spain) in the first ever all-European world heavyweight title clash.

- Undisputed world heavyweight champions **Ingemar Johansen** and **Evander Holyfield** are linked by the fact that they were both disqualified in Olympic boxing tournaments. Johansen was disqualified at the 1952 Games for 'not trying' in the heavyweight final against the American Edward Sanders. Holyfield was disqualified in the 1984 Los Angeles Games for hitting after the break against the New Zealander Kevin Barry in their light-heavyweight semi-final.

- In the late nineteenth century **Charles 'Kid' McCoy** – real name Norman Selby – was one of the great characters of the early days of the sport. The world middleweight champion was not averse to fighting while drunk and taking the odd 'dive'. In 1989 he recorded an impressive victory over heavyweight contender Joe Choynski and one newspaper ran the headline: 'Now you've seen the *Real McCoy*'. A famous phrase was born.

- Naseem Hamed may be unbeaten as a pro but only one Briton has retired as world champion undefeated: **Terry Marsh** won the IBF light-welterweight title in 1987 and was unbeaten in all 27 bouts in his career.

- **Wilfred Benitez** of Puerto Rico became the youngest ever world champion aged just 17 years 176 days, in 1976 when he defeated holder Antonio Cervantes for the WBA light-welterweight title. **George Foreman** was the oldest when he took the WBA/IBF heavyweight titles from Michael Moorer in 1994. Big George, who was also a grandfather, was just short of 46.

- In a 1990 WBC/IBF light-welterweight clash, Mexican legend **Julio Cesar Chavez** was just **two seconds** from defeat when the referee

Richard Steele stopped his opponent **Meldrick Taylor** after 2 min/58 sec of the twelfth round. Taylor was ahead on points at the time.

* In 1976, game Briton **Richard Dunn** challenged **Muhammad Ali** for the world heavyweight title but was knocked out in the fifth round. 'The Greatest' had promised Dunn's manager Mickey Duff his gloves for auctioning after the contest and promptly handed them over in the ring, asking Duff to look inside them . . . he had written 'Ali wins' in one glove and 'KO 5th' in the other before the fight.

* On the subject of **Richard Dunn,** astonishingly the first three world heavyweight title fights staged in Germany featured the first three southpaws to fight for the crown. **Karl Mildenberger** lost to Ali in Frankfurt in 1966 and Dunn lost, as described above, to Ali in Munich. A third southpaw, American **Michael Moorer,** defeated Axel Schulz in Dortmund in 1996.

* **Henry Cooper** is often regarded as the first man to floor 'The Greatest' after his famous 'Hammer' had Ali – or Cassius Clay as he was in those days – on the canvas at Wembley in 1963. However, the previous year **Sonny Banks** had floored Ali at Madison Square Garden only to lose in four rounds.

* 1960s world welterweight and middleweight champion **Emile Griffith** has fought more rounds in world title fights than any other boxer: 339 rounds in over twenty contests.

* Several sets of brothers have held world titles.

However, only one set of twins, **Khaosai and Khaokor Galaxy** of Thailand, have achieved this feat. Khaokor was WBA bantamweight title holder in 1988-89 and Khaosai was WBA super-flyweight king from 1984 to 1991. Khaosai created history by becoming the first fighter to retire having been unbeaten in 20 world title bouts.

- **Larry Holmes** was the only man to fight for the world heavyweight title in the 1970s, 1980s and 1990s. He could uniquely claim to have fought **Muhammad Ali, Mike Tyson and Evander Holyfield** in title contests. Holmes was world champion himself from 1978 to 1985.

- 'We were robbed' is an oft-used phrase by those combatants and spectators who believe they have fallen foul of the sporting fates. Its origins stem from the 1932 world heavyweight title bout when **Jack Sharkey** won the title on points from German **Max Schmeling.** About the bout Joe Jacobs, the manager of Schmeling, uttered the immortal phrase:' We wuz robbed, we shadda stayed in bed.'

- **Muhammad Ali, Joe Frazier and George Foreman** dominated the heavyweight scene in the 1960s and 70s. However, only one man can claim to have fought all three as a professional. Canadian strongman **George Chuvalo** was the first man to take Ali the distance in a world title bout and would later lose to both Frazier and Foreman in non-title contests.

- **Georges Carpentier** of France at 100lb (or just seven stone) was the lightest boxer in history when he began his career in 1908. Astonishingly, in 1922 he would fight **Jack Dempsey** for the world *heavyweight* title (where he weighed in at 172lb) only to lose in four rounds in the first fight to attract a $1million gate. The 'Orchid Man' is a candidate for the finest European fighter of all time, holding European titles at three weights and winning the world light-heavyweight title in 1920.

- The 1974 WBA light-heavyweight clash between **John Conteh** and **Jorge Ahumada** at Wembley created ring history by being the last world title bout to feature just one judge – the referee Harry Gibbs, as was customary in England. All future world title bouts held in Britain were to feature three ringside judges, in line with the rest of the world.

- The controversial draw between **Lennox Lewis and Evander Holyfield** at Madison Square Garden in March 1999 was the first draw in an undisputed world heavyweight title clash for **86 years.** In 1913 **Jack Johnson** held on to the title following a 10-round draw with namesake **Jim Johnson** – the only world heavyweight title fight to feature fighters of the same surname.

- A common misconception is that 1956 Olympic heavyweight champion **Pete Rademacher** is the only reigning champion in history to challenge for a world title, when losing to Floyd Patterson in 1957. **Rafael Lovera** of Paraguay also achieved this feat when he lost to Luis Estaba in a WBC light flyweight title contest in 1975.

- Super-middleweight **Henry Wharton** holds the

unfortunate distinction of being the only Briton to face three other British fighters in world title contests and lose each time. He lost world title fights to **Nigel Benn (1994), Chris Eubank (1994) and Robin Reid (1997).**

Cricket

- A candidate for the most curious first-class match in England has to be the three-day 1982 County Championship match **between Lancashire and Warwickshire** at Southport, when the visitors ran up 523 runs on the first day but were beaten easily by 10 wickets! It featured the following landmarks:
  - On the first day the Warwickshire pair of **Geoff Humpage and Alvin Kallicharran** shared a stand of 448, the highest for the fourth wicket in English cricket.
  - Geoff Humpage hit an English record of 13 sixes in an innings of 254.
  - On the second day, Warwickshire manager **David Brown** became the first substitute to take a wicket in county cricket after replacing Gladstone Small, who was released to play for England.
  - On the final day, the injured Lancashire and England opener **Graeme Fowler** became the first player in cricket history to score two centuries in a match using a runner, who had his hand shaken by a fielder and raised his bat to acknowledge the applause!
  - The final of the Pakistani Quaid-l-Azam trophy in 1959 featured the following score book entry for wicketkeeper Abdul Aziz:

First innings .... Retired hurt 0
Second innings .... Did not bat, dead 0

- **Alec Stewart,** with 6,407 runs, was the leading Test run scorer in the 1990s. **Shane Warne,** with 351 wickets, was the most successful Test bowler of the decade.

- The 2000 blockbuster film *Gladiator* stars **Russell Crowe,** who is the cousin of former New Zealand batting star **Martin Crowe** and captain **Jeff Crowe.**

- The record first-class innings total is 1,107 by Victoria in a Sheffield Shield match against New South Wales in 1926. A month later the two teams met again. Victoria's score? 1,072 runs less, as they made 35 all out!

- Indian test bowler **Madal Lal** suffered a freakish end to his first ever Test innings at Old Trafford in 1974. He was bowled by England's **Mike Hendrick** with the ball knocking both the off and leg stumps out of the ground, leaving the middle stump standing.

- In 1990 **Graham Gooch** became the first man to score over 1,000 Test runs in an English summer, making 306 in three Tests against New Zealand and a record 752 in three matches against India. In making 333 and 123 against India at Lord's, he became the only man in cricket history to record a triple century and century in the same match.

- In the 1997 Ashes Test at Trent Bridge, history was made when, during Australia's first innings, two brothers, **Adam and Ben Hollioake,** were bowling to two brothers, the twins **Mark and Steve Waugh.**

- When England retained the Ashes in Australia in 1970-71, it was the only Test series in history to feature **seven** Test matches, as the third Test of the six-match series at Melbourne was washed out and then replayed as the fifth Test. Curiously, not one of the 99 Australian batsmen dismissed in the series was out lbw . . .

- In 1994 **Brian Lara's** 501 for Warwickshire exceeded by two runs the record score in an innings made by **Hanif Mohammed** in Karachi in 1959. Former South African coach **Bob Woolmer** saw both innings, as a schoolboy in Pakistan and 35 years later as Warwickshire coach. Manchester businessman **Richard Stokes** is believed to have been the only man to have seen both instances of ten wickets being taken by the same bowler in a Test innings, by Jim Laker at Old Trafford in 1956 and the Indian Anil Kumble at Delhi in 1999.

- In the 1999/2000 South Africa versus England Test series captain **Nasser Hussain** became the first player in Test history to bat over 1,000 minutes before being dismissed. After scores of 83 not out (312 mins) and 146 not out (635 mins) he was out after 85 minutes for 15 runs in the fourth Test at Cape Town in January 2000.

- The first ever Test match was held between Australia and England at Melbourne in 1877, Australia winning by 45 runs. In 1977 a special Centenary Test was played at the same venue between the teams. The result? Australia won once again by 45 runs.

- On the opening day of the second Test at Old Trafford on 7 July 1977 (7.7.77), Australian Doug Walters reached 77 not out in the 77th over when his partner was the Australian number 7 Rod Marsh.

- Zimbabwean wicketkeeper **Wayne James** dominated the Matabele against Mashonaland domestic game in April 1996 by achieving two historic and quite different feats. While keeping wicket he equalled the world record when he dismissed nine Mashonaland batsmen in their first innings and then made four more dismissals to set a new world record of thirteen dismissals in a match. When batting he scored 99 and 99 not out in the two innings to become only the second player in history to achieve this unwanted feat.

- A Test match double century is still a rare accomplishment but on 14 March 1999 no less than **four** double centuries were scored in one day in three different Test matches, by **Brian Lara** (213) for West Indies, **Herschelle Gibbs** (211 not out) for South Africa and **Ijaz Ahmed** (211) and **Inzamam Ul-Haq** (200 not out) for Pakistan.

- There have been two tied Test matches in cricket history, Australia against West Indies in Brisbane in 1960 and India against Australia at Madras in 1986. The Lancashire coach in 2000, **Bobby Simpson,** can uniquely claim to have been involved in both matches, as a player in 1960 and as coach to the Australian team in 1986.

- In 1987 Pakistani batsman Javed Miandad made 260 for Pakistan at the Oval against

England. The next eight double centuries conceded by England bowlers were made by Mark Taylor (1989), Aamir Sohail (1992), Vinod Kambli (1993), Allan Border (1993), Brian Lara (1994), Sanath Jayasuriya (1998) and Gary Kirsten (1998 and 1999). **Remarkably all seven of these players, since the right-handed Javed, have been left-handed batsmen.** The list would have been eight had the left-handed Australian opener **Matthew Elliott** not been dismissed for 199 at Headingley in 1997.

- During the first Test against New Zealand at Lord's in 1986, England employed no less than **four** wicketkeepers during their opponents' first innings, following the injury to regular keeper **Jack Richards.** Aside from Richards, batsman **Bill Athey** kept wicket, as did substitutes **Bobby Parks** and former international **Bob Taylor.**

- West Indian legend **Viv Richards** has hit more sixes in Test cricket than any other player, 84 in 121 matches. His colleague **Clive Lloyd** is second with 69 sixes, while not surprisingly **Ian Botham** is the highest-ranking Englishman with 67. West Indian fast bowler **Michael Holding** made just 910 Test runs at an average of 14 but hit a remarkable 34 sixes in his career, leaving him in the top 15 six-hitters in Test history.

- The strangest hat-trick in Test cricket was achieved by **Merv Hughes** for Australia against West Indies at Perth in December 1988. Having dismissed Curtly Ambrose with the last ball of his 36th over and then Patrick Patterson with the first ball of his following over, Hughes had Gordon Greenidge lbw with his first ball of the second innings. At the time nobody noticed the hat-trick had been achieved and it was some time before Hughes was told of his feat.

Football

- Frank Lampard in 1999 became only the third person to follow his father into the full England side. George Eastham Jnr and Nigel Clough are the other two involved, while Eastham also played with his father in the Ards team which won the Irish Gold Cup in 1953-54.

- When Lothar Matthaus played for Germany against Holland in February 2000, he set a new world international record when he gained his 144th cap. It broke former Swedish goalkeeper Thomas Ravelli's previous record of 143.

- Neville Southall (while with Torquay) became only the fifth goalkeeper to reach 700 football league appearances. Peter Shilton (1005), Ray Clemence (758), Pat Jennings (757) and Phil Parkes (743) are the other four.

- At the end of the 1999-2000 season, five players had played League football in each of the last four decades: Tony Ford, Alan Knight, Steve McCall, Nigel Spink and Steve Ogrizovic. Ogrizovic had played in the top flight in each of those decades, with Liverpool and Coventry.

- Only Burnley and Preston have played every season at the same ground since the formation of the Football League in 1888. Strangely, Burnley's opening game in September 1888 was against Preston at Deepdale.

- Jermaine Pennant is the youngest player to play a competitive match for two clubs. He played for Notts County aged 15 years 341 days in December 1998 in an Auto Windscreen Shield game, and then at the age of 16 320 days he turned out for Arsenal in a League Cup tie in November 1999.

- Paul Bracewell lost in four FA Cup Finals – three against Liverpool – while with Everton and Sunderland. However, on the credit side he won championship medals with these four clubs.
  Fulham 1998-99   Divison Two
  Everton 1984-85   Division One
  Newcastle 1992-93   Division One
  Sunderland 1995-96   Division One

- Coventry City last season became the first top-flight side since Leeds in 1992-93 to fail to win an away League game throughout the season. Gary McAllister played in both seasons while Gordon Strachan captained Leeds and managed Coventry.

- Two players last season played for their fifth Premiership club – Carlton Palmer for Sheffield Wednesday, Leeds United, Southampton, Nottingham Forest and Coventry City, and Stan Collymore for Crystal Palace, Nottingham Forest, Liverpool, Aston Villa and Leicester City.

- Craig Burley could have scored a hat-trick of penalties in a game in 1999-2000 for Derby v Bradford City. He scored from two spot-kicks but missed the other. Only Billy Walker (Aston Villa, 1921) Charlie Mitten (Man Utd, 1950) and Ken Barnes (Man City, 1957) have achieved this feat in a top-flight League game.

- Steve McManaman in 2000 became only the 66th player to score in both the European Champions Cup and League Cup Finals. He joined John Robertson (Nottingham Forest), Alan Kennedy (Liverpool), Kenny Daglish (Liverpool) Fabrizio Ravanelli (Juventos and Middlesbrough). McManaman achieved the feat with Real Madrid and Liverpool.

- Edgar Davids is not the first footballer to wear glasses when playing – Alec Raisbeck of Liverpool and Scotland; WS Bourne of West Ham; James Mitchell, Preston's goalkeeper in the 1922 FA Cup Final; Annibale Frossi, who scored twice for Italy in the 1936 Olympic Final; and Van Deale of Feyenoord were others who wore them. But probably the most famous spectacles-wearer was Jeff Jurion, who won 64 Belgium caps and was one of the stars of the great Anderlecht side of the 1960s. Incidentally, the first player to be capped for England while wearing contact lenses was Jack Howe against Italy in 1948.

- Arguably Scotland's best ever side, which beat England 2-0 in 1962, was Brown, Hamilton, Caldow, Crerand McNeil, Baxter, Scott, White, St John, Law and Wilson. With the exception of Billy McNeil, the side comprised players without the prefix of 'Mc' or 'Mac'. Since 1986, John Parrott believes there have been no decent Scotland sides because they've included Ally McCoist!

- In 1930s Herbie Roberts, the Arsenal centre-half, scored a hat-trick but was not exactly applauded off the field. The reason was quite simple – all three goals were own goals and the Gunners were held to a 3-3 draw at Highbury.

- In 1937 Manchester City topped the First Division, but celebrations turned to tears the following year as the club were relegated. They finished as the division's top scorers in the relegation season and actually finished with a positive goal difference (80-77).

- Len Evans (Cardiff and Wales), Steve Heighway (Liverpool and Republic of Ireland) and Don Givens (Man Utd and Republic of Ireland) all made international debuts before appearing in a League game for their respective clubs.

- Danish international Allan Simonsen was the only player to score in the finals of the three major European competitions before the Cup Winners Cup ended in 1999. He netted for Borussia Monchengladbach in the European Cup Final (v Liverpool) in 1997 and for the same club in the finals of the UEFA Cup in 1975 and 1979. He scored for Barcelona in the 1982 European Cup Winners Cup Final.

- By appearing in the Euro 2000 finals, Tony Adams became the first England international to appear in the final stages of international tournaments in three different decades. He played in the European Championship finals of 1988, 1996 and 2000, as well as the 1998

World Cup.

- Brazil and Germany are the only two (out of a possible seven) countries to have won the World Cup who have never played each other in the final stages.

- Only three goalkeepers (Pat Jennings, Ray Clemence and David James) have played for different clubs in Wembley FA Cup Finals. James is the most unfortunate, having failed to win a winners' medal with either Liverpool (1996) or Aston Villa (2000).

- Newcastle made history in 2000 by appearing at Wembley in the FA Cup for a third successive season under three different managers (Kenny Dalglish and Ruud Gullit in the FA Cup Finals of 1998 and 1999 and Bobby Robson in the semi-final in 2000).

- Apart from his successful managerial career, Alex Ferguson also made history by becoming the first ever player to score a hat-trick against Rangers at Ibrox, doing so for St Johnstone in 1963-64. The only player to have since matched this feat is Allan Johnstone of Hearts in 1996-97.

- Ron Atkinson is the only manager to have led three different clubs to victory in major finals at Wembley. He won the FA Cup with Man United in 1983 and 1985 and led Sheffield Wednesday (1991) and Aston Villa (1994) to victory in the League Cup (both games, strangely, against Man Utd).

- Kevin Richardson is the only player to have won the three major domestic honours in England with different clubs. He won the FA

Cup with Everton in 1984, the League title with Arsenal in 1989 and captained Aston Villa to the League Cup in 1994.

- In 2000 the Chelsea pair of Didier Deschamps and Marcel Desailly joined legend Bobby Charlton as the only players to have won FA Cup, European Cup and World Cup winners' medals.

Golf

- Only five golfers have won all five Major titles – **Gene Sarazen, Ben Hogan, Jack Nicklaus, Gary Player and Tiger Woods.**

- There have been only two drawn matches in Ryder Cup history, in 1969 and 1989. Only two men were involved in both matches: **Tony Jacklin and Ray Floyd** as players in 1969 and rival captains in 1989.

- Australian **Brett Ogle** has twice suffered unusual injuries in tournament golf. In the final round of the 1990 Australian Open, when he was just one shot off the lead, he required treatment after a ball he had struck rebounded from a tree, hitting him in the knee. He bravely completed his round limping badly, eventually finishing eighth. At the 1995 Hawaiian Open, at the 13th hole on Friday 13th January, he was hit below the left eye when the shaft of his club shattered after it had caught a tree. He withdrew from the tournament due to blurred vision. Strangely, both tournaments were won by the American **John Morse.**

- At the 1999 Open Championship Australian

Rodney Pampling set an unwanted record by becoming the first golfer in the tournament's history to lead the event after the first round but then to miss the halfway cut, after his first-round 71 was followed by a second-round 86.

- The 1999 Open also saw its youngest ever competitor, 16-year-old English amateur **Zane Scotland.** Sadly, he missed the cut with rounds of 82 and 81. The oldest is **Gene Sarazen** in 1973, see below.

- The two holes-in-one recorded in the 1973 Open at Troon were both made at the famous Postage Stamp hole (the par-3 8th) and coincidentally by the oldest and youngest competitors in the field – the legendary Gene Sarazen (aged 71) and 19 year-old Raymond Russell.

- South African pace legend **Allan Donald** once celebrated taking five wickets in a Test innings against Sri Lanka in 1993 by holing in one at the 320-yard 10th at the Royal Colombo course.

- One of the most spectacular of sporting coincidences happened at the 1989 US Open. Prior to the tournament there had been just 17 holes-in-one at the previous 88 Opens. Then, in less than two hours on the second day of the tournament, at the par-3 sixth, no less than four players, **Doug Weaver, Mark Wiebe, Jerry Pate and Nick Price,** holed their tee shots. The odds on this happening were given at anything up to 8.7 million to one.

- The most holes-in-one by one golfer is believed

to be the 47 by the American amateur **Norman Manley.** Included in this tally is the incredible (and unique) feat of holding in one at consecutive **par fours** at Sangus, California, in 1964. At the opposite end of the scale, one of the greatest golfers of all time, American **Walter Hagen,** who won 11 Majors, recorded just one hole-in-one in his career.

- **Bing Crosby** was a capable golfer who competed in the British Amateur championships. He is one of only two men to have holed in one at famous 16th hole at the Cypress Point course in California, which involves a carry of 180 yards over the Pacific Ocean. His son **Nathaniel** went even better, being US Amateur champion in 1981.

- In 1976 **Maurice Flitcroft,** a golfer with no handicap and only two years' experience, was mistakenly allowed by the organisers to play in the qualifying event for the Open, stating he was an unattached professional. After recording 121 strokes for 18 holes, Flitcroft was shown the door and the Royal and Ancient club vowed to tighten up qualifying procedures. But seven years later Flitcroft was back again, under the pseudonym of Gerald Hoppy from Switzerland, this time recording 63 shots for nine holes before officials intervened. 'Everything was going to plan until I five-putted at the second hole', said Flitcroft. Again officials promised that security would be tightened, but in 1990 Flitcroft was back, this time as James Beau Jolley, only to be thrown out after two hopelessly played holes at the qualifying event at Ormskirk. Flitcroft mused, 'They threw me out before I had warmed up properly.'

- At the Glen Canyon in Arizona, a local ruling states that 'if a ball lands within a club length of a rattlesnake, it may be moved'. The Koolan Island Golf Club in Australia and RAF Waddington GC both have local rules giving right of way to taxiing aircraft. The course at Scott Base in Antarctica uses orange golf balls with snow tunnels as bunkers and allows a free drop if the ball lands in husky droppings!

- The last time the four Majors were not played in their usual order was in **1971,** when the USPGA event was played in February at Palm Beach, Florida, the earliest date on the calendar when a Major has been played. The US Masters was then played in April, followed as usual by the Open and US Open.

- No player has won all four Major championships in the same year. **Ben Hogan** came closest by winning the US Masters, US Open and the Open in 1953. He was denied a chance to win the USPGA as it clashed with the Open at Carnoustie. **Ben Crenshaw** in 1987 was the last player to achieve top-ten finishes in all four Majors in the same year.

- Two men, American **Craig Wood and Greg Norman,** have lost in play-off in all four Major championships. Wood was the first to set this unenviable record between 1933 and 1939. Norman lost all four of his play-offs between 1984 and 1993. **Tom Watson** is the only player to lose in play-offs in consecutive Majors, doings so at the 1978 USPGA and the 1979 US Masters.

- On a happier note for **Greg Norman,** he is the only player to have twice carded rounds of 63 – the lowest on record – in Major championships. His second round of 63 at Turnberry in 1986 led to his first Major, while his first round 63 at the 1996 US Masters preceded his spectacular collapse against Nick Faldo in the final round.

- **Nick Faldo** won more Major championships (four) in the 1990s than any other player. His nearest challenger was **Nick Price,** whose three included back-to-back wins at the 1994 Open and USPGA, the last time this feat was achieved prior to Tiger Woods' achievements in 2000.

- TV commentator **Ewen Murray** was World Junior golf champion in 1971.

- Irishman **Padraig Harrington** was disqualified from the Benson and Hedges International Open in 2000 in the last round for failing to sign his card from an earlier round, thus losing out on a possible £166,000 first prize. Older spectators may have remembered Argentinian #Roberto de Vicenzo missing a play-off at the 1968 US Masters when he mistakenly signed for a par 4 (instead of his actual birdie 3) at the penultimate hole.

- In 1977 it was discovered that the clubs with which **Tom Watson** had won his first three Major championships were illegal, having irregular grooves. However, no retrospective action was taken.

Horse Racing

- In 1947 Timeform established its handicap of all horses running in Great Britain, along with many of the more prominent horses trained overseas. On the Timeform Handicap, the best rated horse (at 145lb) was Sea Bird, the 1965 Derby and Arc winner. Secretariat, Ribot and Brigadier Gerard were the next best rated horses. Mill Reef was eighth, Nijinsky 15th and Shergar 18th.

- The top-rated British/Irish Hurdler of the twentieth century was Night Nurse, the Champion Hurdle winner in 1976 and 1977.

- The top-rated steeplechaser of the last century was three times Cheltenham Gold Cup winner Arkle. Desert Orchid was rated fifth and Mill House, Arkle's great rival, sixth.

- The longest odds winner of the 2,000 Guineas in the last century was Rockavon (66-1), the only Scottish-trained winner of the race, which won in 1961.

- Harry Wragg was the only person to win both the 1,000 Guineas and 2,000 Guineas as both jockey and trainer in the twentieth century.

- Winners of English Classics on a
  disqualification since 1900:
  Known Fact 2,000 Guineas 1980 – Nureyev
  disqualified
  Aboyeur Derby 1913 – Craganour
  disqualified
  My Dear Oaks 1918 – Stonyford disqualified
  Snow Bride Oaks 1989 – Aliysa disqualified

- Sinndar in 2000 became the first Irish-trained
  Epsom Derby winner since Secreto in 1984.

- Signorinetta (1908) and Aboyeur (1913) both
  won the Derby at odds of 100-1.

- Pawneese in 1976 was the only horse to win
  the Epsom and French Oaks.

- Between 1975 and 1999, Henry Cecil set a
  twentieth-century record by training 22
  English Classics, one more than Alec Taylor
  (1905-1927)

- Lester Piggott has ridden a record 30 English
  Classics and was the only man to ride a
  Classic winner in each of the last five decades
  of the twentieth century.

- Istabraq in 2000 became the fifth horse to
  win three successive Champion Hurdles, the
  last to achieve this feat having been See You
  Then in 1987.

- The mare Dawn Run was the first horse to
  win both the Cheltenham Gold Cup and
  Champion Hurdle.

- In 1999 Paul Carberry rode the first Irish
  winner of the Grand National since 1975,
  when his father Tommy Carberry had brought

L'Escargot home. Paul's winning horse Bobby Jo was trained by Tommy.

- In 1999 Richard Dunwoody retired after riding 1699 career winners, the most ever in National Hunt history. Dunwoody, though, also took 669 falls in his career, a quite frightening tally.

Motor Racing

- 1998 and 1999 world champion **Mika Hakkinen** is the only driver to have driven for the same team in over 100 Formula One races. He joined McLaren as replacement for Michael Andretti in 1993 and reached this landmark with the team in 2000.

- **Graham Hill** is the only driver to have won the Formula One drivers' title (1962 and 1968), the Indianapolis 500 (1965) and the Le Mans 24 Hour race (1972).

- Flying Finn **Keke Rosberg** holds the distinction of being the only driver to win the world drivers' title (in 1982 for Williams) after failing to score a point in the previous season. In 1981 he had failed to trouble the scorers when driving for former world champion Emerson Fittipaldi's team.

- No British woman has driven in a world championship race, although former Olympic skier **Divina Galica** did compete in the 1977 non-title 'Race of Champions' at Brands Hatch. **Lella Lombardi** is the only woman to have scored points, finishing sixth in Spain in 1975. In 1980 Lombardi would partner **Mark**

Thatcher (son of former Prime Minister Margaret) at the Le Mans 24 Hour race.

- Motor racing is a well-known haven for the rich and famous. Screen legend **Paul Newman** finished second in the 1979 Le Mans 24 Hour race driving a Porsche and **Steve McQueen** was second for Ferrari in the 1970 World Championship Sports Car race at Sebring in the USA; he had entered with the intention of using footage from the race for his film Le Mans.

- Britain's **Jenson Button** became the first teenager to score points in Formula One when he finished sixth in the 2000 Brazilian GP. The previous record holder had been Ricardo Rodriguez of Mexico, who was 20 years 4 months when fourth in the 1962 Belgian Grand Prix.

- The fastest ever Formula One Grand Prix was the Italian race at Monza in 1971, the winner (Britain's **Peter Gethin**) averaging nearly 151 mph for the race. The race also featured the closest ever blanket finish: the first five drivers were separated by just over **half a second!**

- The smallest margin of victory is an amazing one-hundreth of a second when **Ayrton Senna** pipped **Nigel Mansell** at the 1986 Spanish Grand Prix.

- **Alain Prost** holds the record for winning his home Grand Prix more times than any other driver. The four times world champion recorded **six** victories in the French Grand Prix between 1981 and 1993.

- **Andrea de Cesaris** has the unfortunate

distinction of competing in a record 208 Formula One races without a victory. His best finish was second on two occasions. TV commentator **Martin Brundle** holds the British record, with 158 races being punctuated by three second places.

- Three times world champion **Jack Brabham** is the only driver in history to win Formula One Grand Prix races in three different decades, recording his first victory at Monaco in 1959 and his last in South Africa in 1970.

- World champions **Emerson Fittipaldi** (first title 1972), **Jody Scheckter** (1979) and **Michael Schumacher** (1994) all competed in Formula One races against their brothers. **Wilson Fittipaldi** drove for a couple of seasons in the early 1970s, **Ian Schecter** drove in 18 races in the late 1970s and of course, **Ralf Schumacher** began his Formula One career in 1997.

- The **Wolf** team in 1977 were the last constructors to win their first ever Grand Prix when **Jody Scheckter** won the Argentinian Grand Prix. The year before, Scheckter had driven a Tyrell to victory in the Swedish race; nothing unusual in that apart from the fact it was the only Grand Prix won by a car with six wheels!

- **Graham and Damon Hill** are the only father and son combination to have both won the world drivers' title. The closest matching this feat were **Jacques Villeneuve,** who won the title in 1997, and his late father **Gilles,** who was second in the 1979 championship.

- The closest finish to the World Drivers'

Championship was in 1984 when **Niki Lauda** was champion by just half a point from **Alain Prost.**

- Four drivers have won the American Indy Car Championship and Formula One drivers' title: **Mario Andretti, Emerson Fittipaldi, Nigel Mansell and Jacques Villeneuve.**

- The great **Jim Clark** won 25 Grands Prix in his career but incredibly finished second only once, in Germany in 1963.

- The **1961 Dutch Grand Prix** at Zandvoort will probably remain unique in Grand Prix history as the only race where all the cars finished. There were also no pit stops during the race!

- At the opposite end of the scale, the 1996 Monaco Grand Prix saw just three cars finish. Wet conditions meant that the three podium drivers, **Olivier Panis (first), David Coulthard (second) and Johnny Herbert** were the only survivors.

- Since the first Formula One race in 1950, only Italian **Giancarlo Baghetti** has recorded a victory in his first ever Grand Prix, doing so in France in 1961.

Olympics

- The only man to win gold medals in both Summer and Winter Games was Eddie Eagan (USA), who won the 1920 light-heavyweight title in boxing and was a member of the 1932 winning four-man bob team.

- The heroes of the award-winning film Chariots of Fire were British Olympic gold medal winners of 1924 Harold Abrahams (100m) and Eric Liddell (400m).

- When Lord Burghley won the 1928 Olympic 400 metre hurdles, he became the first member of the British House of Lords to win an Olympic athletics title.

- The 1928 Olympic Games turned out to be a goldmine for Hollywood talent scouts. Johnny Weissmuller (Tarzan), Buster Crabbe (Buck Rogers), Eleanor Holm, a leading lady, Herman Brix (Tarzan) and Sonja Henie, the famous ice skater, became famous stars on the screen.

- When the Czechs won the silver medal in 1948 in the ice hockey, a member of the team was Jaroslav Drobny, who six years later won the Wimbledon men's singles title.

- When Josy Bathel won the Olympic 155 metres title in 1952, the band had trouble finding his national anthem. Barthel had gained Luxembourg's first, and still their only, gold medal.

- Ivan Ossier (Denmark) in the fencing competition and Magnus Konon (Norway) in the yachting events both competed in two Olympic Games in London. They created a record as the Games were held 40 years apart in 1908 and 1948.

- The 1956 Summer Olympics began on 10 June in Stockholm and ended in Melbourne on 8 December 1956. The equestrian events, due to the stringent Australian quarantine laws, had to be held in Sweden, while the rest of the Games went ahead as usual for the first time in the southern hemisphere.

- Great Britain's modern pentathlon team won the Olympic 1976 gold medal when Boris Onischenko (URS) was discovered to have tampered with his épée in the fencing segment of the competition and was disqualified.

- The 1972 basketball competition caused a sensation when official RW Jones of Great Britain gave the Soviet team an extra few seconds at the end of the final game, during which they scored the winning points to take the title by 51-50. They thus ended America's remarkable run of 63 consecutive victories in Olympic basketball since its introduction in 1936. The defeated Americans refused the silver medal and to this day the medals remain in a bank vault and the wills of the players state they shall never be reclaimed by any member of their families.

- Tiny Liechtenstein have won just four medals in Olympic competition – all in the Winter Games and by two people from the same family. Hanni Wenzel won both women's slaloms and took silver in the downhill in 1980, while brother Andreas also won a silver medal.

- John Kelly, the 1920 single sculls rowing champion, was the father of actress Grace Kelly, who later became the Princess of Monaco. Coincidentally, these were the first Games at which Monaco had participated.

- The best punch thrown by featherweight Valentin Loren (Spain) at the 1964 Tokyo Olympics cost him suspension for life from amateur boxing. After being disqualified for repeated fouling, the Spaniard hit the referee with a perfectly timed left hook and then launched a vicious punch at a Netherlands judge, who, in kindness, was endeavouring to calm the Spaniard.

- Flyweight Don-Kih Choh (South Korea) at least didn't take his anger out on the referee in the same Games after his disqualification for throwing a punch after the referee had called 'stop'. The boxer staged a sit-down strike for nearly one hour before being cajoled into leaving the ring.

- In Paris in 1924, Eugen Lunde won a sailing gold medal; in 1952 his son Peter Lunde won a yachting silver, while in 1960 Eugen's grandson, also Peter Lunde, won gold in the Flying Dutchman competition. They became the first father, son and grandson to have won Olympic medals.

- Vyacheslav Ivanov (USSR) was so delighted when he won the single sculls at Melbourne (1956) that in his excitement he threw his gold medal into the air. He failed to catch it and it disappeared into the waters of Lake Wendouree. Ivanov dived in to reclaim it to no avail and professional divers followed suit. The IOC later presented him with another medal, and the Russian retained his title four years later in Rome.

- A member of Hungary's World Championship-winning shooting team, Karoly Takac, lost his right hand when a grenade exploded in 1938. He then taught himself to shoot with his left and won the Olympic rapid five gold medal in 1948 and 1952.

Rugby League

- When Sheffield Eagles became probably the biggest surprise winners of the Challenge Cup in 1998, it was Denis Betts' first defeat in 35 Cup outings. Betts had previously won seven successive winners medals (1989-94) before going to New Zealand to play.

- Jason Robinson in 1998 became the first player to score a try in each match of a three-Test series against both Australia Super League and New Zealand.

- In 1996 Wigan lost in the Challenge Cup for the first time after a run of 43 successive ties won. Shaun Edwards was the only player to appear in all 43 including once as a substitute.

- Paul Loughlin played in five Wembley Finals and lost on all five occasions. He lost with St Helens three times and then with Bradford in 1996 and 1997 against . . . St Helens.

- Loughlin's team mate Bernard Dwyer played in two of St Helens' defeats, in 1989 and 1991, and for Bradford in 1996 and 1997. His luck changed in 2000 when he finally won a winners' medal against Leeds.

- In 2000 Henry Paul followed his brother Robbie (1996) in winning the Lance Todd Trophy for the Challenge Cup Final's man of the match. Neil Fox (1962) and brother Don (1968) had previously achieved this distinction.

- Between 1990 and 1997, Bobbie Goulding played in five Challenge Cup Finals – for three sides, Wigan, Widnes and St Helens. In that time he also played for Great Britain while at Leeds.

- Leroy Rivett in 1999 became the first player to score four times in a Challenge Cup Final at Wembley. His club Leeds beat London 35-16, a record win.

- Between 1980 and 1990 inclusive, Widnes' Mike O'Neill won six Premiership winners' medals with the club. Martin Offiah also won six medals – three with Widnes and three with Wigan.

- No player had scored a hat-trick of tries in the Premiership Final until 1995. Then two Wigan players, Kris Radlinski and Gary Connolly, achieved the feat against Leeds.

- The legendary Alex Murphy captained St Helens (1966), Leigh (1971) and Warrington (1974) to Challenge Cup Final wins. On the last two occasions he was player-coach.

- Two players have been sent off in Challenge Cup Finals at Wembley – Syd Hynes (Leeds, 1971) and Richie Eyres (Widnes, 1993).

- In 1992 on the Great Britain tour to New Zealand and Australia, Wigan provided 13 players plus David Myers as a replacement – a record by any club.

- Since the war, only three sets of brothers have been on British touring sides – Don and Neil Fox (1962), Alan and John Bates (1974) and David and Paul Hulme (1988).

- In 1985-86 Joe Lydon became the first £100,000 player when he joined Wigan from Widnes.

- Jeff Grayson and son Paul played rugby league together at Bradford Northern.

Rugby Union

- MJK Smith made just one appearance for England in 1956 at fly half against Wales. His cricket career lasted a lot longer, as he captained his country 25 times and made 50 Test appearances.

- The legendary Welsh full back JPR Williams won the Junior Wimbledon tennis title before making 55 appearances for Wales in his chosen sport. He played for Wales in three decades, from 1969 to 1981.

- The first player to be sent off in an international was New Zealand's Cyril Brownlie in 1925 against England. It was 42 years before another player suffered the same fate and again it was an All Black – Colin Meads against Scotland.

- The third player to be sent off was Englishman Mike Burton in 1975 against Australia.

- Ian McCrae was the first replacement in an international when he came on for scrum half Gordon Connell for Scotland against France in January 1969. Three months later England's first substitution saw Keith Fielding, replaced by Tim Dalton, who never played again for his country.

- In February 1974 fly-half Alan Old played for England at Murrayfield while his brother Chris played for England in the West Indies on the same day. Unfortunately, both played in defeated sides.

- Nigel Melville had the unusual distinction of captaining England on his debut, doing so in 1984 against Australia. Irishman Rob Saunders in 1991 and Welshman Mike Watkins in 1984 also achieved this feat.

- In 2000 Austin Healey became only the third Englishman to score a hat-trick in the International Championship since 1924. John Carleton (1980 v Scotland) and Chris Oti (1988 v Ireland) were the others.

- Federico Mendez in 2000 became the first player to win a European Cup winners' medal with different clubs. He came on as a replacement in the 1998 final for Bath and then played in 2000 with Northampton.

- Zimbabwean player Richard Tsimba scored a try in the 1987 World Cup against Romania and performed a somersault in going over the line between the posts. However, it caused him an injury and curtailed his own further participation in the competition.

- When France played New Zealand in July 1961, France fielded the two Boniface brothers while the All Blacks selected the Clarke brothers Don and Ian and the brothers Mead, Colin and Stan.

- Erica Roe in 1982 was the first woman to streak at Twickenham, or course, but to commemorate the 'feat' she released a record called 'Remember Then'. It failed to make the charts.

- After South Africa's 44-0 demolition of Scotland in 1951 at Murrayfield, a local journalist muttered 'and they were lucky to get none' – and a famous sporting phrase was born.

- Canada's Gareth Rees is the only player to have appeared in all four Rugby World Cups.

- Strangely, although he won 72 international caps for England, Will Carling won only one cap for the British Lions, on the 1993 tour to New Zealand.

- The Calcutta Cup, the annual match between England and Scotland, is so named because it was made in India from the rupees left in the bank by the disbanded Calcutta Club in 1876.

- The first captain of the British Lions, Robert Seddon, drowned in an accident on their tour of Australia in 1888.

Snooker

- Stephen Hendry lost only three times in the World Championship in the 1990s – to Steve James in 1991 in the quarter-final, Ken Doherty in the 1997 final and then Jimmy White in 1998.

- Jimmy White's defeat of Hendry in 1998 was even more remarkable because White was a qualifier.

- John Higgins in 1998 compiled the first hat-trick of century breaks since the World Championship went to Sheffield in 1977. During the course of the fortnight, Higgins amassed 14 century breaks, another record.

- In 1997 Ronnie O'Sullivan became the fourth player in World Championship history to compile a 147 break. Cliff Thorburn (1983), Jimmy White (1994) and Stephen Hendry (1995) were the others. O'Sullivan, who earned £165,000 in total for the feat, compiled the break in just five minutes and 20 seconds.

- In December 1998 John Parrott won the German Masters, and in so doing completed tournament wins in nine countries.

- No first-time world champion has ever retained his title at Sheffield.

- In the Benson and Hedges Masters in 2000, Ken Doherty failed to pot the black and missed the chance of only the second 147 in that championship. Kirk Stevens remains the only player to achieve this feat, in 1984.

- In the 2000 World Championships, John Higgins scored a Crucible record of 485 points without conceding one in the game against Anthony Hamilton.

- In 1997 not one Englishman reached the Crucible semi-finals. Stephen Hendry, James Wattana, Ken Doherty and Alain Robidoux made up the quartet, while in 2000 the occurrence was repeated as Mark Williams, Matthew Stevens, John Higgins and Joe Swail reached the last four.

- The only whitewash in the World Championships was in 1992 when John Parrott defeated Eddie Charlton 10-0 in the first round.

- Mark Williams received £240,000 when winning the 2000 World Championship. The winner of the first final at the Crucible in 1977, John Spencer, received £6,000.

- Terry Griffiths won the world title at his first attempt in 1979. He is the last player to do so. Only three others, Joe Davis, John Spencer and Alex Higgins, won the championship in their debut season.

- Probably the two biggest surprises at the Crucible concerned the two dominant figures.

In 1982 Tony Knowles defeated reigning champion Steve Davis 10-1 in the first round while in 2000 Stephen Hendry was eliminated 10-7 at the same stage by virtual unknown Stuart Bingham. Bingham had had to win four matches just to qualify for the final stages.

- Tai Pitchit, a qualifier for the Crucible in 1995, is the competitor with the longest name. A former Buddhist Monk, his real name is Chuchart Triratt Anapradit!

- The famous 1985 World Final between Dennis Taylor and Steven Davis produced the highest TV audience in snooker history with 18.5 million watching. This remains a record for any sports programme on the BBC – and for any broadcast after midnight.

Tennis

- In 1973, 79 members of the Association of Tennis Professionals boycotted the Wimbledon championships after Nikki Pilic of Yugoslavia was suspended. Three players defied the call to boycott: Roger Taylor (Great Britain), Ille Nastase (Romania) and Australian Ray Keldie.

- When Rod Laver became the highest earning men's player in the first year of the 'open' era in 1969, he earned an estimated $124,000. Andre Agassi in 1999 earned just a little more – $4,269,265.

- Australian-born Gail Sheriff won the French women's doubles championship under three different identities – in 1967 as Miss Gail Sherriff, in 1970 and 1971 as Mme JB Chanfreau and in 1976 as Mme J Lovera.

- The legendary Australian Davis Cup captain Harry Hopman's wife Nell won the Australian mixed doubles in 1930 with Harry, and the French women's doubles in 1954 with Maureen Connolly.

- At the end of 1999, only two left-handed

women had won the Wimbledon singles title – Ann Jones and Martina Navratilova.

- Ken Rosewall played in four Wimbledon singles finals and lost all four. Two were in the Fifties (1954 and 1956) and the other two in the Seventies (1970) and 1974).

- Jaroslav Drobny competed in the Wimbledon championships under four different national descriptions:
1938 and 1946-49 Czechoslovakia
1939 Bohemia – Moravia
1950-1956 Egypt
1960 Great Britain

- Between 1993 and 2000, Pete Sampras won seven Wimbledon singles titles. The only player to defeat him in that time was Richard Krajicek, who went on to win the 1996 Final.

- Krajicek in 1996 became only the second unseeded winner of the Wimbledon men's singles after Boris Becker in 1985. Krajicek defeated American Mal Washington, who was also unseeded.

- Einer Ulrich played 28 Davis Cup ties for Denmark from 1924 to 1938. His sons Torben and Jorgen then followed him into the team. Torben played 40 ties and Jorgen 24, making the Ulrichs the most capped family with 80 ties from 1924 to 1977.

- Hans Redl played Davis Cup for Austria in 1937 against Germany. Following Hitler's annexation of Austria, Redl played for Germany in 1938 and 1939. Following the war, he played again for Austria – but with one major difference. He had lost his left arm on military service and as a result the service rule in tennis was changed with the clause 'A player with the use of only one arm may utilize the racket for projection'.

- Martina Navratilova is the only woman to win the Wimbledon singles while representing two countries – Czechoslavakia and then the USA.

- Dr Renee Richards was defeated in both the men's and women's singles in the US Championships! In 1960, under the name of Richard Raskin, he lost to Neale Fraser and in 1977, after a sex change, she lost to Virginia Wade.

- In 2000 Mary Pierce became the first French woman to win the French singles since Françoise Durr in 1967.

- In winning the 2000 French men's doubles, Mark Woodforde and Todd Woodbridge won their 58th career double title breaking McEnroe/Fleming and Hewitt/McMillan's previous record of 57 titles.

- Big Bill Tilden, the greatest player of the 1920s, had already won major titles when he lost part of the middle finger of his racket hand. The American's career seemed over as he held the racket with virtually his finger tips. However, he adjusted his grip as best as he could and went on to dominate the game for some years after.

- Big Bill was involved in one of the great comebacks in tennis history, although he was on the receiving end. In the 1927 Wimbledon semi-final he was two sets up and 5-1 ahead but somehow lost to Henri Cochet 2-6, 4-6,

7-5, 6-4, 6-3.

- Andre Agassi won all four grand slam titles during the 1990s. The only player to appear in the final of all four events in the nineties was Jim Courier, who won the French and Australian titles but was beaten in the final at Wimbledon and the US Open.

- Yevgeniy Kafelnikov, when winning the men's singles and doubles titles at the 1996 French Open, became the only man since Stefan Edberg (at the Australian Open in 1997) to achieve this double at a grand slam event.

- Since the Challenge Round was abolished in 1992, only two men have appeared in seven men's singles finals at Wimbledon. They are Boris Becker and Pete Sampras.

- Hana Mandlikova was the only woman to play both Martina Navratilova (1985) and Chris Evert (1981) in singles finals at Wimbledon, unfortunately losing on both occasions.

- In 1999 the American Alexandra Stevenson became the first qualifier to reach the ladies singles semi-final at Wimbledon. She lost at this stage to eventual champion Lindsay Davenport.